Christmas 2001

Robert —

Merry Christmas!

Much Love

Kenneth

NEW YORK
CITY

IN PHOTOGRAPHS 1850 – 1945

NEW YORK CITY

IN PHOTOGRAPHS 1850–1945

BY SUSAN WRIGHT

Barnes
&Noble
BOOKS
NEW YORK

Title page (overleaf): Aerial view of Manhattan, 1945 (NATIONAL ARCHIVES)

PHOTO CREDITS

MUSEUM OF THE CITY OF NEW YORK

Since its founding in 1923, the Museum of the City of New York has
amassed an outstanding collection of objects related to the history of
New York City. This collection—as vibrant and eclectic as New York
itself—numbers 1.5 million objects and forms the heart of the museum's critically acclaimed exhibitions and publications, its programs for
children, adults, and families, and its research services. The
Photographic Collection alone includes more than 500,000 images
documenting New York City, beginning in the mid-nineteenth century,
including substantial holdings of the work of Berenice Abbott, the
Byron Company, Irving Underhill, Jacob Riis, and the Wurts Brothers.

THE NEW-YORK HISTORICAL SOCIETY

The New-York Historical Society was founded in 1804 and has since
collected a vast range of visual materials that illuminate the history of
New York City and America. These collections have proved invaluable
to historians, documentary filmmakers, architects, novelists, artists,
teachers, and many others. The scope of the society's 75 separate collections, with one million items, includes not only New York's past but
also the nation's, through photographs, posters, and advertisements.

COPYRIGHT

1999 Barnes & Noble Books

ISBN 0-7607-1274-3

Book design by Patti Ratchford

Printed in Hong Kong

99 00 01 02 MC 9 8 7 6 5 4 3 2 1

C&C

CONTENTS

ACKNOWLEDGMENTS

In preparing this book, I looked at more than 20,000 photographs of New York City, in a dozen private and public collections. Narrowing the selection down was difficult, and some notable New York landmarks have regrettably been left out.

All of the photographs included in this book were taken between 1850 and the end of World War II, the dawn of the modern era for New York and the world. Each was chosen because it tells a story about a particular time and place.

They are not intended to present a comprehensive history of New York, but instead offer a photographic glimpse of the people and places that contributed to the exciting evolution of one of the world's great cities.

I would like to thank John Kelly, Rick Campbell, Lynne Arany, Jessi Fiechter, Rick Willett, and Patti Ratchford for their collaboration and inspiration in creating this book.

I would also like to thank the collections for their help in providing photographs: The Museum of the City of New York, The New-York Historical Society, The National Archives, The Brooklyn Public Library, The Bronx County Historical Society, The Queens Historical Society, Archive Photos, The Everett Collection, The Howard W. Frank Collection, William C. MacKay, and Time Life Syndication.

The dates used in this book correspond to those given in *The Encyclopedia of New York City,* the excellent one-volume reference edited by Kenneth T. Jackson (New Haven: Yale University Press, 1995). I've also included a bibliography of the many fine books and historical documents that served as sources.

SUSAN WRIGHT

NEW YORK CITY

IN PHOTOGRAPHS 1 8 5 0 – 1 9 4 5

INTRODUCTION

First, biggest, and best are superlatives that are repeatedly used when recounting New York City's history. It started out as a tiny European settlement, but by the end of World War II it was the second largest city in the world, growing to a size second only to London in area and population in less than 300 years.

How did New York do this? Diversity helped. Some people find the city's variety of people, buildings, and cultural activities overwhelming. But much of New York City's vitality was gained through immigration: people came from all over the world to live, work, and prosper here. The character and customs, the drive and energy of their distinctive neighborhoods have made New York what it is today.

Another reason for New York City's success can be summed up by the real estate mantra: location, location, location. The group of islands at the mouth of the Hudson River on the eastern seaboard offers one of the best natural harbors in the world. The area also has a temperate climate and there were plenty of fertile rolling hills suitable for the early farmers.

The first Europeans to sight New York were Giovanni da Verrazano and his men in 1524, but the Italian explorer never set foot on land. Henry Hudson was the first to thoroughly explore the area, hoping that he had discovered the fabled waterway of the Northwest Passage. Hudson reported to his employers at the Dutch East India Company that he

AERIAL VIEW OF DOWNTOWN

Battery Park, at the tip of Manhattan, separates the Hudson piers on the left from the East River piers. The skyscraper heights in Lower
Manhattan dip toward the marshy regions of the Lower East Side and Greenwich Village. Skyscrapers rise again in the distance, in Midtown.

RETURNING FROM EUROPE, 1945

During World War II, New York City became the port of embarkation for the American Expeditionary Forces sailing for France. Nearly 900,000 New Yorkers wore uniforms in the service of America during the war. Here, the city welcomes back 5,000 soldiers returning from Europe.

(NATIONAL ARCHIVES)

had encountered Indians wearing luxurious beaver and otter fur, and by 1625 New Amsterdam was established. In the beginning, the settlement served as a trading post between the Dutch and the Indians.

From the first few hundred families, the Dutch influence in the area has echoed through New York history. The early settlers changed the shape and size of the islands by draining and filling marshy land and tidal areas. They also built homes like those in Holland with a raised first floor and a high stoop in front. This style of structure is still common in New York, even though the risk of flooding is negligible compared to the Dutch homeland.

The English took over New Amsterdam without a shot in 1664 after the Dutch West India Company went bankrupt. The Dutch colony was renamed New York in honor of James Stuart, the Duke of York (who later became King James II). The Dutch and English among the 1,500 inhabitants got along well, so business basically went on as usual even with the change in sovereignty.

During the American Revolution, New York City was occupied by the British. George Washington ordered the transfer of the American forces to New York because he felt that control of New York was key to winning the war. Washington saw that if the British were successful in taking control of the Hudson River, they would split the colonies, cutting off New England from the South.

Nearly one-third of the battles in the Revolutionary War took place in and around New York City. American troops didn't regain the city until 1783, when the British finally fled. New York became the nation's capital and stayed so from 1785 to 1790, when it was moved to Philadelphia, before settling finally in Washington, D.C. George Washington was inaugurated at Federal Hall, in New York City, as the first president of the United States on April 30, 1789.

Between the Revolution and the Civil War, New York City grew as the premier port of the United States. New York merchants served as the middlemen for English manufacturers and American farmers after the completion of the Erie Canal in 1825, which connected the Hudson River to the Great Lakes. Manhattan businesses controlled well over half of the nation's imports and more than one-third of its exports.

New York was the most powerful city in the nation when Abraham Lincoln was elected president. Ultimately the city's business was stimulated by the Civil War, and New York enjoyed a burst of postwar prosperity in manufacturing and in new banks and insurance firms. Immigration, transportation, and communication became the keys to increased wealth in New York and in America.

When Greater New York was chartered in 1898, joining the boroughs of Manhattan, Brooklyn, Queens, the Bronx, and Staten Island, the population totaled three and a half million people. New York was now an important financial, manufacturing, and cultural center of the world. The city became renowned for its fine newspapers, restaurants, theater, and fashion. It was home to the advertising and publishing industries, and many fine universities in the area contributed to its growing fame.

The city is much more than an infrastructure of landmarks, buildings, businesses, parks, and transportation systems. The people of New York have created and re-created their unique environment over and over again, through tenacity and innovation. E. B. White described New Yorkers as "to a large extent strangers who have pulled up stakes somewhere and come to town, seeking sanctuary or fulfillment or some greater or lesser grail."

It is New York's strength—in a city where the only constant is change—that it thrives on the different influences and cultures that its newcomers bring.

This is why New York has become the world's greatest city.

THE BAY OF NEW YORK, BATTERY PARK, 1894

This view of the harbor shows Battery Park in the foreground with Governors Island in the distance. The southernmost park in Manhattan was named Battery Park because of the series of forts constructed there by the Dutch and the British. On Governors Island, the round fort called Castle Williams was completed in 1811. (ARCHIVE PHOTOS)

THE STATUE OF LIBERTY

The Statue of Liberty was envisioned by French statesman Edouard René de Laboulaye; sailing into New York for the first time, Laboulaye wrote of his idea for a statue to commemorate liberty and friendship between the two nations: "The surfaces should be broad and simple, defined by a bold and clear design, accentuated in the important places." Sculptor Frédéric-Auguste Bartholdi modeled the statue. Liberty's upraised hand rises some 395 feet above the water; her thumbnail alone is nearly a foot long. The statue was brought over from France in pieces and reassembled on tiny Bedloe's Island in New York Bay in 1886. (ARCHIVE PHOTOS)

THE CITY GREETS ARRIVING DIGNITARIES, CA. 1930

New Yorkers always did things bigger, better, and bolder than ever before. This photograph shows the extraordinary reception parade that greeted royalty, statesmen, and conquering heroes on their approach to America. Tugs, fireboats, fishing scows, and steamships escorted the vessel into New York Bay while blowing their horns to announce the arrival. The city even had an official reception boat, the MACOM.

(J. HAL STEFFEN/COLLECTION OF THE NEW-YORK HISTORICAL SOCIETY)

ELLIS ISLAND FERRY STATION (above)

The most modern structure on Ellis Island was the ferry house, built in 1935 by the Public Works Administration. Ferryboats brought New Yorkers to Ellis Island so they could be reunited with immigrating relatives at the now famous "kissing post." Immigrants who passed the inspection were transported via ferry to Manhattan, where they were dropped off to fend for themselves. (NATIONAL ARCHIVES)

ELLIS ISLAND, 1934 (facing)

Ellis Island, originally known as Oyster Island, was New York's immigration station from 1892 until 1954. The complex had a recreation room, a library, and a kindergarten, with a dormitory that held 1,000 beds. In the peak year of 1907, 1,285,349 immigrants were admitted to America; by 1924 more than 16 million immigrants had passed through Ellis Island. (NATIONAL ARCHIVES)

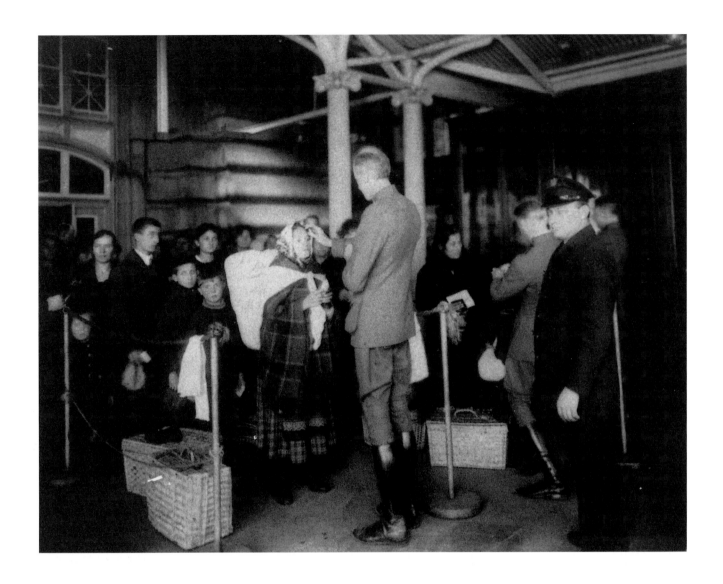

INSPECTING IMMIGRANTS ON ELLIS ISLAND

Diseases fouled the air of steerage from the close contact and the filth that accumulated during the stormy Atlantic passage. Many people arrived seasick and exhausted, in need of medical attention. More than 98 percent of the prospective immigrants gained entry to America, and it took eight hours for more than 80 percent to be processed. The 2 percent who didn't pass the inspection were put on ships and returned to their country of origin. On one voyage in 1882 from Amsterdam, 1,155 steerage passengers endured the trip, with an average of 16 people to a room. It was considered remarkable that only five passengers died during the voyage. (NATIONAL ARCHIVES)

IMMIGRANTS ARRIVING IN NEW YORK ON THE SS POTSDAM, CA. 1900

Engraved on the pedestal of the Statue of Liberty is Emma Lazarus's now famous poem that includes the phrase, "Give me your tired, your poor, your huddled masses yearning to breathe free." (COLLECTION OF THE NEW-YORK HISTORICAL SOCIETY)

M A N

LOWER

HATTAN

ew York City began in Lower Manhattan. From the initial purchase of the city from the Native Americans to its first sky-scraper, the region from the Battery north to 14th Street was the center of New York life for its first 200 years, and it has continued to be a hub of economic and cultural activity ever since.

By the time of the American Revolution, Wall Street was the center of New York fashion, and the social elite lined the cobblestone street with their fine houses. By the mid-nineteenth century, the tenor of the neighborhood had shifted, as businesses increasingly crowded out families. Wall Street became the financial center, not far inland from the busy docks where merchandise changed hands.

Originally an Indian path running from the Battery to present-day City Hall Park, Broadway was at one time lined with two rows of shade trees, making the broad avenue a favorite place for people to stroll. But as more and more important and innovative buildings went up there, and businesses continued to build northward at the rate of about one mile each decade, Broadway became the main north-south route in Lower Manhattan, reaching 14th Street in 1840.

During the population explosion of the early nineteenth century, wooden houses were hastily constructed in the marshy district later known as the Lower East Side. The immigrants who moved there tended to cluster according to their countries of birth and to retain many of their cultural traditions, adding immeasurably to the spirit and liveliness of the city.

At the turn of the century, the Italian section known as Little Italy was centered around Mulberry Street. The Bowery separated it from the Jewish quarter, while the adjoining Chinatown district lay to the east on Mott and Pell Streets.

Some of the poorer districts in New York were slums. Charles Dickens went into the New York slums in 1842, describing "these narrow ways diverging to the right and left, reeking everywhere with dirt and filth."

Greenwich Village was a refugee boomtown during the yellow fever epidemic of 1822, when Wall Street businessmen moved north into the pure air. Since 1811, when Village residents resisted the Grid Plan, which mandated the neat crisscrossing pattern of streets in much of the borough, Greenwich Village has been known for defying authority, and as a home to socialists, suffragettes, philosophers, writers, and avant-garde artists.

Political unrest, social reform, breakthroughs in art and architecture, the development of one of the world's great stock exchanges—all are part of the colorful and groundbreaking history of Lower Manhattan.

FRAUNCES TAVERN, CA. 1900
Built in 1719 as a private residence, Fraunces Tavern on Pearl and Broad Streets survived both historical upheavals and natural disasters. The tavern was bought by the Sons of the Revolution in 1904 to preserve the site of George Washington's farewell to the officers of the American Revolution. It reopened in 1907 with a restaurant and the Fraunces Tavern Museum. (COLLECTION OF THE NEW YORK HISTORICAL SOCIETY)

CASTLE GARDEN IN BATTERY PARK, CA. 1900

Between 1855 and 1890 nearly eight million immigrants entered America through this round former fort with eight-foot walls, which was called Castle Garden. When Ellis Island was chosen as the new receiving station in the late nineteenth century, Castle Garden was converted into an aquarium, and was a popular tourist attraction from 1896 to 1941. (ROBERT L. BRACKLOW/COLLECTION OF THE NEW-YORK HISTORICAL SOCIETY)

BOWLING GREEN EXCAVATION FOR THE CUSTOMS HOUSE, CA. 1905

According to legend, Governor Peter Minuit of New Amsterdam was standing on Bowling Green (visible just above the excavation pit in this photograph) when he "bought" Manhattan in 1626 from Native Americans. It was New York's first—albeit tiny—public park. The Customs House was completed in 1907 for the offices of the Collector of Customs of the Port of New York. (GEORGE P. HALL & SON/ COLLECTION OF THE NEW-YORK HISTORICAL SOCIETY)

TRINITY CHURCH ON WALL STREET, CA. 1875

Wall Street was originally residential, as seen in this photograph of Trinity Church from Nassau Street. The original church burned down in 1776 and was rebuilt in 1790. The second church was torn down and replaced in the 1840s with this English Gothic Revival church made of locally quarried brownstone. The church was the tallest structure in Manhattan until the Pulitzer Building surpassed it in 1892. (ROEGE N.Y./MUSEUM OF THE CITY OF NEW YORK)

WALL STREET AT THE TIME OF THE CRASH, 1929 (above)
Many investors speculated in securities using borrowed money. Black Tuesday hit on
October 29, 1929—the beginning of the panic and subsequent crash of the market. In
the next few days, in spite of strategic buying by American banks to restore confidence,
investors were unable to cover their margins and lost their holdings. (EVERETT COLLECTION)

OLD STOCK EXCHANGE BUILDING, CA. 1897 (facing)
By 1792, 24 brokers had begun trading stocks and government securities under an old
buttonwood tree at 68 Wall Street. This picture shows the first permanent headquarters
of the New York Stock Exchange, on Broad and Wall Streets. The exchange building was
replaced at this same site in 1903; J. P. Morgan and Co. headquarters was across the
street. (ROBERT L. BRACKLOW/COLLECTION OF THE NEW-YORK HISTORICAL SOCIETY)

"BUY MY APPLES," CA. 1930 (right)
Millions of people lost their jobs during the Great Depression that followed the crash.
Nearly nine million savings accounts were wiped out, 85,000 businesses went bankrupt,
and 5,000 banks failed. (IRVING BROWNING/COLLECTION OF THE NEW-YORK HISTORICAL SOCIETY)

LOEW FOOTBRIDGE OVER BROADWAY, CA. 1867

HARPER'S described Broadway as "not only a channel of commercial traffic, but a favorite promenade of the idler and pleasure-seeker, and though the acquaintances of a man be few, a walk up or down Broadway is sure to confront him with someone that he knows." Crossing Broadway was so hazardous that a footbridge was built across the avenue. The bridge was torn down a year after this photograph was taken because Knox the Hatter claimed it obstructed the light to his store and attracted disreputable loiterers. The corner of Astor House can be seen on the upper right—the most famous New York hotel in the early nineteenth century. (ARCHIVE PHOTOS)

BROOKLYN BRIDGE AND STREETS OF LOWER MANHATTAN, 1892

This photograph was taken from the balcony encircling the dome of the World Building on Park Row. The former New Amsterdam colony grew naturally, with only a few public buildings planned for designated sites, while the more numerous private dwellings were built wherever it was convenient for the early settlers. In 1811, the city adopted a grid plan that guided the development of streets in Manhattan, but it did not affect most of Lower Manhattan. (ROBERT L. BRACKLOW/COLLECTION OF THE NEW-YORK HISTORICAL SOCIETY)

SOUTH STREET NORTH TO THE WOOLWORTH TOWER, CA. 1900
Despite the nearby skyscrapers in Lower Manhattan, the waterfront continued to dominate South Street. The street connected the docks with government buildings and the merchants who served the shipping industry. Chandlers sold seamen supplies like sou'westers, pea jackets, and dungarees. Local hotels and bars offered cheap food, drink, and lodging. (ROBERT L. BRACKLOW/COLLECTION OF THE NEW-YORK HISTORICAL SOCIETY)

THE BLIZZARD OF 1888, NEW STREET LOOKING TOWARD WALL STREET
Julian Ralph of the NEW YORK SUN reported on the legendary blizzard that began on Monday, March 12, 1888: "The wind fell upon the house sides in fearful gusts, it strained great plate glass windows, rocked the frame houses, pressed against the doors so that it was almost too dangerous to open them." Many of the 40 to 90-foot utility poles collapsed in the gale, paralyzing the city. Some were bisected by up to 30 double cross-arms and strung with 300 separate wires. After this disaster, the utility wires were finally buried underground. (BROWN BROTHERS/ MUSEUM OF THE CITY OF NEW YORK)

THE EQUITABLE BUILDING ON FIRE, 1912

Over the years, terrible fires swept through the densely packed warehouses and offices of Lower Manhattan, dramatically changing the face of the city. In 1912, the headquarters of the Equitable Life Assurance Society caught fire and was completely destroyed. The building "yielded up its seared and worldly soul," according to the NEW YORK DAILY TRIBUNE. The skyscraper that replaced it was so massive that city planners decreed that all future skyscrapers had to incorporate a stepped-back design to allow light and air to enter the city. (FREDERICK HUGH SMYTH/COLLECTION OF THE NEW-YORK HISTORICAL SOCIETY)

TO THE RESCUE, 1904

For more than a 100 years the city was protected by volunteer firemen armed only with leather buckets. The first two fire engines, Newsham hand pumpers, arrived in New York in 1731. By the mid-nineteenth century, there were 64 companies, each with 26 volunteers. Young men were tempted to join the volunteer companies because firemen played a crucial role in politics, and because there was a tremendous sense of company pride. The professional Metropolitan Fire Department was established after the Civil War. (FREDERICK HUGH SMYTH/COLLECTION OF THE NEW-YORK HISTORICAL SOCIETY)

FROZEN WATER HANGING FROM THE EQUITABLE BUILDING, 1912

Getting enough water to put out fires was not an easy task for the firemen. It was said in 1837: "There is not perhaps in the Union a city more destitute of the blessing of good water than New York." The need for a good supply of water prompted New Yorkers to approve the Croton Aqueduct System. (FREDERICK HUGH SMYTH/COLLECTION OF THE NEW-YORK HISTORICAL SOCIETY)

HOLD IT RIGHT THERE! CA. 1900 (above)

In this photograph, a traffic violator is being stopped by a policeman on a bicycle. Theodore Roosevelt created the police bicycle squad in 1895 when he was appointed president of the City Police Board. (NATIONAL ARCHIVES, PICTURES OF THE AMERICAN CITY)

TERMINAL, PARK ROW AND BROADWAY, 1892 (facing, above)

Alfred Stieglitz's photograph of a horse-drawn streetcar in New York City appeared in CAMERA WORK, no. 36, in 1911. The first streetcars began running in 1832, usually with straw strewn on the floor and only one small kerosene lamp illuminating the interior. The horsecar companies were assured of their contracts from Tammany Hall, so the public vehicles were in disrepair and were rarely cleaned. "New York has to put up with the horsecars because it is against the law to operate overhead trolleys," an official of the Metropolitan Street Railway Company said in the NEW YORK DAILY TRIBUNE shortly before electric streetcars took over. "If that statute was not written in the law books, it would not be three months before every horsecar in the city was broken up for junk. Electric cars, with brilliant lights and buzzing trolleys, would be running over the cross-town and belt lines." In 1908 all horse-drawn streetcars were retired. (ALFRED STIEGLITZ/NATIONAL ARCHIVES, PICTURES OF THE AMERICAN CITY)

BROADWAY OMNIBUS, CA. 1870 (facing, below)

Broadway was traversed from Bowling Green to 14th Street, and later further uptown, by means of public omnibuses. These carriages operated from the 1830s until 1885. The passengers entered through a high door at the rear, an awkward endeavor for a lady in long skirts. Passengers signaled the driver to stop by pulling on a leather strap attached to his leg. (COLLECTION OF THE NEW-YORK HISTORICAL SOCIETY)

TRIAL TRIP OF THE FIRST ELEVATED RAILROAD, 1867 (above)
Charles T. Harvey wore formal attire for the first test run of his experimental elevated railroad. The cars were pulled by a cable connected to a steam-powered generator. The half-mile track was erected 30 feet above Greenwich Street, from the Battery to Dey Street. In 1875, the city appointed a rapid-transit commission that selected Second, Third, Sixth, and Ninth Avenues as the routes for the first elevated railroads. (MUSEUM OF THE CITY OF NEW YORK)

EARLY RAILWAY TRACKS, 1891 (facing, above)
In 1832 the first rail tracks were laid through the streets to make it easier for horses to pull the streetcars. By 1890 there were at least 24 railway firms in the city, each running a route or branch. This photograph shows the tracks turning onto Canal Street, named for the stream that ran from Collect Pond to the Hudson River. Canal Street later became the main east-west traffic artery across Lower Manhattan, connecting the Manhattan Bridge from Brooklyn to the Holland Tunnel leading to New Jersey. (ROBERT L. BRACKLOW/COLLECTION OF THE NEW-YORK HISTORICAL SOCIETY)

THE "EL" AT COENTIES SLIP FROM PEARL STREET, 1889 (facing, below)
In this photograph of the snake curve of the elevated railroad at Coenties Slip, you see the modern technology of telegraph wires and the Third Avenue "El" as well as the more traditional wooden carts and sailing ships. (ARCHIVE PHOTOS)

SUBWAY CONSTRUCTION, CA. 1900 (above)
Soon after London opened the first underground railroad system in 1863, New Yorkers recognized the need for a subway in their city. Mark Twain described the streets as "a torrent of traffic," while THE NEW YORK TIMES criticized Governor Fenton, saying: "There is not enough room on the surface of the city to accommodate the traffic which its business requires." (ROBERT L. BRACKLOW/COLLECTION OF THE NEW-YORK HISTORICAL SOCIETY)

DIGGING THE SUBWAY, 1925 (facing, above)
The Rapid Transit Subway Construction Company was awarded a $35 million contract in 1900 to construct the subway. Twelve thousand laborers set to work blasting trenches in the solid rock of Manhattan Island. The subway workers earned $2 for a ten-hour day; many were from the tenement districts. In 1904, the first subway train left City Hall Station for Grand Central Station, where it then crossed Midtown to Times Square before proceeding up the West Side to 145th Street. The ride cost a nickel. (EVERETT COLLECTION)

STRAPHANGERS, CA. 1940s (facing, below)
In time, New York City's subway system developed into the most heavily traveled passenger railroad in the world, carrying five and a half million passengers every day. The fare in 1945 was still a nickel. (MUSEUM OF THE CITY OF NEW YORK)

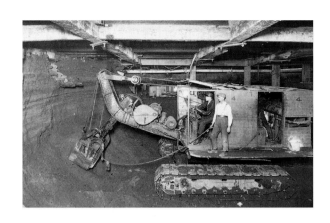

NEW YORK WORLD STAFF WRITERS, CA. 1905
The WORLD served New York City by fighting Tammany corruption,
exposing the graft that occurred daily in city government. The newspapers
were so successful that by the turn of the century, 25 New York dailies
were thriving, as well as Yiddish, Italian, and German dailies. Here, the
city staff of the WORLD endeavors to get out the next edition in its
cramped City Office. (COLLECTION OF THE NEW-YORK HISTORICAL SOCIETY)

LINOTYPE ROOM OF THE NEW YORK WORLD,
CA. 1905
The printing presses are being readied. The famous St. Louis reporter
Joseph Pulitzer bought the NEW YORK WORLD from Jay Gould in
1883. Pulitzer and his rival, William Randolph Hearst, brought a
combination of excitement and entertaining vulgarity to journalism.
The rivalry of the two papers using a blend of fact and gossip is
often considered to be the birth of "yellow journalism." (COLLECTION
OF THE NEW-YORK HISTORICAL SOCIETY)

NEWSPAPER BOY, 1912

This issue of the EVENING NEWS announces the sinking of the TITANIC and the loss of more than 1,500 lives. The Cunard liner CARPATHIA rescued the surviving passengers and transported them to New York City. (ARCHIVE PHOTOS)

ANTI-HITLER PROTEST IN FRONT OF CITY HALL, 1933

City Hall has been the site of a number of historic events, such as this anti-Hitler protest in which more than 100,000 people marched to protest Hitler's ascent to power in Germany. The City Hall building was considered to be one of the most beautiful structures in New York. Pure white marble faced the harmonious blend of French Renaissance and American Colonial design. But the north side of the building was left in plain brownstone. Since the entire city was south of City Hall when it was completed in 1812, the City Council thought it wouldn't be worth the expense of marble facing on the rear, which "would be out of sight to all the world." (NATIONAL ARCHIVES)

TAMMANY HALL, 14TH STREET, 1868

The Society of St. Tammany began in 1788 as a benevolent fraternal and patriotic organization. By the 1840s, Tammany was actively helping arriving immigrants find work, thus gathering their votes to form a powerful political base. In 1868, when Tammany Hall was completed, it hosted the Democratic National Convention. Combined with the New York County Democratic Committee, Tammany Hall proved so powerful that the colossal political machine held New York in the palm of its hand well into the twentieth century. (EVERETT COLLECTION)

BOSS TWEED

William Marcy Tweed, known as Boss Tweed, controlled the New York State capital and courts through his grip on Tammany Hall. Tweed rewarded those who pleased him with prestigious jobs, expensive contracts, and influential government appointments. By 1869, he was stealing more than $1 million a month from the city treasury and was one of the city's largest landowners. Under fire, Tweed was expelled from the Tammany Society in 1871, and in 1873 he was sentenced to 12 years in prison. (MUSEUM OF THE CITY OF NEW YORK)

THE MAYOR HELPS OUT DURING A STRIKE, 1945

Fiorello La Guardia, mayor of New York from 1933 to 1945, was renowned for his charm, generosity, and the unpretentious life he lived with his family in an apartment in Harlem on upper Fifth Avenue. This photograph shows La Guardia as many New Yorkers remember him—reading DICK TRACY on July 8, 1945 over the radio during a newspaper strike. (ARCHIVE PHOTOS)

NINE HUNDRED TRUCKS MOBILIZED AT CITY HALL TO COUNTER THE TEAMSTERS' STRIKE, 1938

City Hall was the site of protests and gatherings as well as city-sanctioned actions. Mayor La Guardia was making a visible statement when he ordered the Department of Sanitation to mobilize 900 trucks during a teamsters' strike. La Guardia had offered to settle with a wage increase for the 15,000 teamsters, but they refused. The mayor used nonunion men and city trucks to bust the strikers. (EVERETT COLLECTION)

HIZZONER EXPRESSES AN OPINION, CA. 1935

Mayor Fiorello La Guardia was best known for his dedication to ridding the city of corruption, chasing crooks, closing burlesque houses, and cracking down on gambling, including this public display of smashing slot machines and pinball machines. (ARCHIVE PHOTOS)

THE BIRTH OF THE SKYSCRAPER, CA. 1907

On its completion in 1908, the 47-story Singer Building at 149 Broadway was the tallest building in the world. Beyond the Singer tower is the City Investing Company Building, also under construction. The City Investing Building was one of the first to have the masonry stepped-back design that was typical at the turn of the century. Architect Ernest Flagg created the first modern skyscraper in the slender tower of the Singer Building. (FRANK M. INGALLS/COLLECTION OF THE NEW-YORK HISTORICAL SOCIETY)

PHOTOGRAPHERS ON THE ROOF OF THE SINGER TOWER, CA. 1908

Until the seven-and-a-half-story Equitable Building was completed in 1870, none of the buildings in New York were taller than six stories. Higher structures were quickly constructed as elevators were improved. (ARCHIVE PHOTOS)

WOOLWORTH BUILDING, 1938

Frank W. Woolworth asked architect Cass Gilbert to design the Woolworth Building like the British Houses of Parliament. The 60-story Gothic structure even included gargoyles at the top, which led to the Woolworth Building being nicknamed "the cathedral of commerce." Woolworth owned 684 "five and dime" stores, yet he had been turned down for a loan by the Metropolitan Life Insurance Company. In revenge, he paid cash to commission the tower, and in order to "humble" the Metropolitan Life Building on Madison Square in Midtown, he made sure his building was taller. The Woolworth Building on Broadway was the tallest building in the world when completed in 1913. (EVERETT COLLECTION)

REACHING FOR THE SKY, CA. 1935

As skyscrapers grew more gigantic in the 1930s, new engineering problems arose. Unusual wind resistance was created by the tall structures, so models had to be placed in wind tunnels to test the reaction of the materials. Most skyscrapers "rocked" from five to 15 centimeters, but the motion couldn't be detected by people inside. In this photograph, a newer skyscraper, the Cities Services Building, constructed on Pine Street, is shown surpassing the height of the older Woolworth Building in the background. (IRVING BROWNING/COLLECTION OF THE NEW-YORK HISTORICAL SOCIETY)

GOVERNOR AL SMITH AS PRESIDENTIAL NOMINEE, 1928

The city held a ticker-tape parade to celebrate the nomination of Democratic New York Governor Al Smith for president; Smith, a Catholic, had grown up in the slums of Manhattan's Lower East Side. His rise to prominence was aided by the Tammany machine. Smith was elected governor of New York four times before his nomination for president in 1928. He lost the election to Republican Herbert Hoover. (EVERETT COLLECTION)

WELCOME HOME, TEDDY, 1910

Theodore Roosevelt was a popular native New Yorker from a well-to-do family who, after a stint in the New York State Assembly and on the City Police Board, served as governor of New York, until he was elected vice president in 1900. He became president in 1901, after William McKinley's assassination. In 1909 Roosevelt left office and traveled extensively abroad. On his return to the United States in June 1910, his shop docked at New York City and he was greeted with a ticker-tape parade of unprecedented size. (MUSEUM OF THE CITY OF NEW YORK)

PARADE FOR CHARLES LINDBERGH, 1927

Charles Lindbergh's triumphant return from Paris was celebrated with a ticker-tape parade after he made the first nonstop flight over the Atlantic in the SPIRIT OF ST. LOUIS. Accompanying the young hero in the parade was New York Mayor Jimmy Walker, the Tammany-appointed playboy who was one of the most popular mayors the city ever had. Walker was famous for writing the popular song, "Will You Love Me in December Like You Do in May?" (ARCHIVE PHOTOS)

SAILBOATS DOCKED AT NEW YORK HARBOR, CA. 1900
By 1840, New York was second only to London among ports in the world. New York tradesmen owned more than one-fifth of all the registered American tonnage. Clipper ships were developed in the mid-nineteenth century; long, narrow ships with tall sails could travel faster than traditional sailing ships. The result was a dramatic increase in trade. (ROBERT L. BRACKLOW/COLLECTION OF THE NEW-YORK HISTORICAL SOCIETY)

SOUTH FERRY TERMINAL AND BARGE OFFICE, 1931
South Ferry next to Battery Park was the site of the busy Staten Island Ferry Slip and the ferries to Coney Island and Rockaway Beach. Customs cutters departed from the Barge Office to meet incoming transatlantic ships, so reporters often gathered here to get the first ship's news. The Battery was also the traditional berthing spot for important visitors, where New Yorkers gathered to welcome celebrities, heroes, and visiting politicians. This photograph shows an official procession leaving the pier to march along Battery Park toward Broadway for yet another celebratory ticker-tape parade. (EVERETT COLLECTION)

COVERED DOCKS NORTH OF THE BROOKLYN BRIDGE

Many of the larger East River piers were also enclosed freight depots. The smaller slips were used by ferries carrying passengers to Brooklyn, Queens, and Lower Manhattan. (RUDOLPH SIMMON/MUSEUM OF THE CITY OF NEW YORK)

THE BROOKLYN BRIDGE WITH AN OCEAN LINER

The battered hull of the old ship next to the rotting wooden pier contrasts with the majestic sweep of the Brooklyn Bridge and an ocean liner. New York City grew so fast that it became increasingly difficult to transport people and goods by water. The Brooklyn Bridge was the first suspension bridge to traverse the river, eventually replacing the ferry lines. (MARK NADIR/NATIONAL ARCHIVES)

OYSTER HOUSEBOATS, SOUTH STREET AND PIKE SLIP, 1937

These houseboats, built in the 1860s and moored under the Manhattan Bridge, sold oysters to local restaurants and hotels. The boats were privately owned until the city took possession of them in the 1930s. (BERENICE ABBOTT/MUSEUM OF THE CITY OF NEW YORK)

LOADING ICE ON THE NEW YORK DOCKS, CA. 1932 (above)
Ice was delivered to the docks, where it was used to preserve food. All of the fish that were brought into the Fulton Fish Market were cleaned and packed in ice. (SOL LIBSOHN/NATIONAL ARCHIVES)

THE VIEW FROM THE PIERS AT SOUTH STREET, CA. 1900 (facing, above)
With the financial district as a backdrop, South Street was the center of maritime affairs on the Lower Manhattan waterfront. The long shorelines of both the Hudson and the East River were monopolized by trade and shipping interests, while the pursuit of investment revenue was the focus of commerce further inland among the financiers. (ROBERT L. BRACKLOW/COLLECTION OF THE NEW-YORK HISTORICAL SOCIETY)

SAILORS UNLOADING FISH (facing, below left)
The Fulton Market on South Street, established in 1822, was the largest wholesale fish market in the United States, selling up to a million pounds of fish every day. Before daybreak, tons of fish were unloaded from the holds of trawlers, then packed in ice to be transported to market. (DAVID ROBBINS/NATIONAL ARCHIVES)

STEVEDORES LOADING BARRELS, CA. 1912 (facing, below right)
Barrels of corn syrup were stacked on the dock, while discharging inspectors superintended the transfer of the cargo from the ship. All goods had to be carefully weighed, gauged, measured, and checked off the manifest. Cargo remained at the dock or in a public warehouse until the proper permits had been approved and were obtained by the owner. (LEWIS HINE/NATIONAL ARCHIVES, PICTURES OF THE AMERICAN CITY)

BOYS CLIMBING A CRANE

New York was the last large American city to establish public schools. Even after public schools were opened in the nineteenth century, only one-third of the pupils who enrolled at the elementary level graduated from the eighth grade. Children often lived in the streets, ran in gangs, and worked in the factories or as messenger boys. Most children lied about their age, with even the smallest pathetically pledging to be 14, the legal age for working. (AUBREY POLLARD/NATIONAL ARCHIVES)

CHILDREN'S PLAYGROUND, 1898

Private benevolence funded children's playgrounds in the tenement districts on the Lower East Side, in Hell's Kitchen, and in Harlem. A "playground" was generally an empty dirt lot, occasionally with a sandbox or swing set. In 1895 a city law stipulated that "hereafter no schoolhouse shall be constructed in the city of New York without an open-air playground attached to or used in connection with the same."

CHILDREN PLAYING IN THE TENEMENTS

The Work Projects Administration commissioned a project on Lower East Side children called "One-Third of the Nation." The writers and photographers found children who lived in the streets, day and night, with hardly any supervision. Often children looked out for one another, with small boys and girls tending even younger children. (ARNOLD EAGLE AND DAVID ROBBINS/NATIONAL ARCHIVES)

CHILDREN SLEEPING ON MULBERRY STREET, 1890

One nineteenth-century survey estimated that at least 30,000 children lived on the streets. "The Street Arab has all the faults and all the virtues of the lawless life he leads," wrote Jacob Riis in his influential book HOW THE OTHER HALF LIVES. "Vagabond that he is, acknowledging no authority and owing no allegiance to anybody or anything, with his grimy fist raised against society whenever it tries to coerce him, he is as bright and sharp as a weasel, which, among all the predatory beasts, he most resembles." (THE JACOB A. RIIS COLLECTION/MUSEUM OF THE CITY OF NEW YORK)

THE CHERRY HILL GANG IN MULLEN ALLEY, 1888

Gangs terrorized the city, waging street battles and giving New York City the reputation of being the most wicked city in the world. This photograph shows the gang in front of Mullen Alley, seven feet wide at the near end and narrowing to less than two feet further in. The MORNING JOURNAL described Mullen Alley in 1888: "Twenty-five or 30 families, most of them having many children, live in each of the two houses between which it lies. Two wretched rooms, with one window for each room, form the home of every family." (THE JACOB A. RIIS COLLECTION/MUSEUM OF THE CITY OF NEW YORK)

BANDITS' ROOST ON MULBERRY STREET, 1887

Journalist Jacob Riis used documentary photographs such as this one to illustrate HOW THE OTHER HALF LIVES. Riis discovered that photographs of the tenements and street children conveyed the dreadful truth of conditions on the Lower East Side much better than written reports. He investigated the city's worst slums, populated by immigrants who had little choice in where they could afford to live. Gangs were born in the tenements, fighting for turf and any type of money-taking they could get away with in the crowded city. (THE JACOB A. RIIS COLLECTION/MUSUEM OF THE CITY OF NEW YORK)

INSPECTION OF A CLUTTERED BASEMENT
APARTMENT, CA. 1900
A Citizens' Association was formed to regularly send physicians and
inspectors to examine the tenements. The inspectors reported they found
disease, polluted milk and water, and rats who were plumper and livelier
than the children living in the narrow, windowless rooms. (NATIONAL
ARCHIVES, PICTURES OF THE AMERICAN CITY)

REAR OF A TENEMENT ON ROOSEVELT STREET,
CA. 1890
Often the toilets of the tenement buildings were in the backyard and
rusty pipes brought cold water to a single tap in the kitchen. The
prejudice against immigrants was reflected in the building codes; as late as
the 1920s, opponents of private bathrooms in tenements argued that
inhabitants would "only put coal in the bathtub." (THE JACOB A. RIIS
COLLECTION/MUSEUM OF THE CITY OF NEW YORK)

SHANTIES CROWDED BY THE "BEEHIVE," CA. 1872
Inspectors claimed that over 1,000 Italians lived in the cluster of eight tenements
on Baxter Street known as the "Beehive." The newly built tenements, behind the
old shanties in this photograph, were the subject of complaints about bad smells to
the Board of Health. A sanitary inspector followed the stench into the cellar.
Digging around one of the pipes, he discovered that it simply ran into the ground
and was not connected to the city's sewer system. (THE JACOB A. RIIS
COLLECTION/MUSEUM OF THE CITY OF NEW YORK)

AIR SHAFT OF A DUMBBELL TENEMENT, CA. 1900
By 1900, more than one and a half million New Yorkers were living in slums. The
Lower East Side was the most densely populated area in the world. New York's
poor people paid more rent while living under worse conditions than poor people
in any other American city. The "dumbbell tenement" was named for the shape of
its airshaft, which was intended to bring light and air into the stifling interiors of
the crowded buildings. (NATIONAL ARCHIVES, PICTURES OF THE AMERICAN CITY)

FIGHTING TUBERCULOSIS ON THE ROOF, CA. 1890

Tuberculosis contributed to the high death rate in densely populated areas with poor hygienic standards. During the last two decades of the nineteenth century and the early twentieth century, the treatment for tuberculosis was fresh air, rest, relaxation, and special diets. (THE JACOB A. RIIS COLLECTION/MUSEUM OF THE CITY OF NEW YORK)

PARADISE PARK AT FORMER MULBERRY BEND, CA. 1900
Ten years of angry protests and reform efforts finally convinced city authorities to level the condemned tenements and shanties
on Mulberry Bend. Two new parks were created to ensure there were a few open spaces in the slums. (JACOB A. RIIS COLLECTION/
MUSEUM OF THE CITY OF NEW YORK)

THE DREADED MULBERRY BEND, CA. 1890
Jacob Riis called Mulberry Bend the most dangerous place in the city. The poverty was extreme—in the 1860s a census of
the Bend found that only 24 out of the 609 tenements were in decent condition. The street and the ever-present corner saloon
provided the only social life for residents. Three-fourths of the population of the so-called "Bloody Sixth" Ward were then Irish,
but by the 1880s Italians had moved into the area, which became known as Little Italy. (JACOB A. RIIS COLLECTION/MUSEUM OF
THE CITY OF NEW YORK)

MOE LEVY & COMPANY, 1911
Many immigrants were either unskilled or unable to speak English, so they worked on construction jobs or in sweatshops. New York City was famous for its garment industry, built on the back of cheap labor. Hours were long and conditions unsanitary, with the workers relatively powerless to oppose the exploitation. (THE BYRON COLLECTION/MUSUEM OF THE CITY OF NEW YORK)

ELDRIDGE STREET SYNAGOGUE
The Eldridge Street Synagogue was the first great house of worship designed and built by Jews from Eastern Europe, in 1887. Before this synagogue existed, immigrants had worshipped in converted churches and small storefront spaces. Membership began to dwindle in the 1920s as residents relocated and U.S. immigration limits changed. (COURTESY OF THE ELDRIDGE STREET SYNAGOGUE)

THE ELEVATED TRACKS ON THIRD AVENUE
The "El" tracks, built in 1878, ran close by the tenements on narrow Third Avenue. People living on the second and third floors had no privacy unless the shades were pulled down. Windows were kept tightly closed to prevent squirting oil from splattering into parlors and bedrooms. (ARCHIVE PHOTOS)

THE CENTER OF YIDDISH THEATER, CA. 1930S

Second Avenue from Houston north to 14th Street was known as the Jewish Rialto. Yiddish theater in America is a unique blend of Jewish legends and traditions, and is as old as the first Russian immigrants. It was said that the diet of poor Jews was "bread smeared with theater." Two generations later, the Second Avenue Theater was still popular, with Molly Picon appearing in ABI GEZUNT. The actress's career was reputedly boosted in 1929 when her rendition of a Yiddish ballad brought tears to Al Capone's eyes. (ARCHIVE PHOTOS)

FOOD SHOPPING

Between 1881 and 1910 nearly one and a half million Jews fled the Russian empire. Many settled in New York City, around Hester, Essex, and Ludlow Streets. Because it was difficult for them to get jobs outside the Jewish neighborhood, they set themselves up as independent merchants, traders, professionals, and clothing manufacturers. (NATIONAL ARCHIVES)

PEDDLERS AT THE CORNER OF RIVINGTON AND ORCHARD STREETS, CA. 1930

The Orchard Street pushcart market was famous for fruits, vegetables, bagels, clothing, and other dry goods. In THE NEW METROPOLIS (1899),
E. Idell Zeisloft estimated that 1,500 Jewish families relied on the pushcart for a living because little capital was required to go into business.
On Saturdays the streets were cleared of pushcarts, and thousands of orderly people in their best Sabbath-day clothes strolled to the synagogues.

CHINATOWN, CA. 1930

In 1872, there were only 12 Chinese people living on Mott Street, but by World War II, the community of Chinese immigrants in the neighborhood of Mott and Pell Streets had swelled to 4,000 residents. (IRVING BROWNING/COLLECTION OF THE NEW-YORK HISTORICAL SOCIETY)

DOYERS STREET FROM THE BOWERY, CHINATOWN, CA. 1920

Chinese immigrants were restricted to only a few kinds of work, including hand laundries, shops, and tourist attractions. THE WPA GUIDE TO NYC described one shop as containing "hexagonal and fluted green bowls, native spoons of China, simple brown paper fans, packets of joss sticks, sturdy black cotton slippers without backs, strangely shaped but unusually durable toothbrushes, beautiful green-leafed Chinese lilies, wall pockets for flowers, long-handled wooden back-scratchers." (W. J. ROEGE/COLLECTION OF THE NEW-YORK HISTORICAL SOCIETY)

MANHATTAN BRIDGE, 1937

Traffic congestion on the Brooklyn Bridge was eased with the completion of the Williamsburg Bridge in 1903 and the Manhattan Bridge in 1909. These three bridges were modern marvels of architecture, and carried more than 750,000 commuters between Manhattan and Brooklyn. The Manhattan Bridge joined with Canal Street near the Bowery in the heart of Chinatown. The triumphal arch and curved colonnade were inspired by Bernini's baroque colonnade in the Piazza of St. Peter's in Rome. (RUDOLPH SIMMON/MUSEUM OF THE CITY OF NEW YORK)

CHINATOWN AT NIGHT, 1939

This photograph, taken with a time-elapse camera, was taken six months after a disastrous fire raged through the heavily populated Chinese district. In a few short months, repairs were made and the neighborhood was as busy as ever. (NATIONAL ARCHIVES)

McSORLEY'S OLD ALE HOUSE

Established in 1854 at 15 East Seventh Street, McSorley's was one of nearly 8,000 saloons in the city. The pub was a favorite place for students enrolled in the Cooper Union and Peter Cooper himself often joined them to discuss intellectual subjects. (ARCHIVE PHOTOS)

COLONNADE ROW

A row of spectacular residences known as Colonnade Row was completed in 1833 on Lafayette Street just below Astor Place. The fashionable Greek Revival design of the houses was unified by a two-story colonnade that had 27 Corinthian columns. This view shows only four of the original nine houses that were left standing after 1902. The homes were occupied by society families and visited by notables such as Washington Irving, Charles Dickens, and Peter Cooper. (ROBERT L. BRACKLOW/MUSEUM OF THE CITY OF NEW YORK)

TOM THUMB'S WEDDING, 1863

On February 10, 1863, thousands of New Yorkers thronged Grace Church at Broadway and East 10th Street to witness the wedding of Charles Stratton, P. T. Barnum's "Tom Thumb," and the equally diminutive Minnie Warren Bump. Attending were governors, generals, congressmen, and millionaires. Detained by the Civil War, President Lincoln could not be present, but he did send Chinese fire screens as a wedding gift. (COLLECTION OF WILLIAM C. MACKAY)

Mr. & Mrs. General Tom Thumb

TEMPORARY WASHINGTON ARCH, 1889

For the centennial celebration of Washington's inauguration, Stanford White created an imposing wooden arch that spanned Fifth Avenue north of Washington Square Park. The arch was lit with hundreds of the new incandescent lights and hung with festive wreaths and garlands. It was so popular that a permanent white marble arch was later placed inside the park. The permanent arch was a replica of Stanford White's design except for the small statue of Washington on top. (COLLECTION OF THE NEW-YORK HISTORICAL SOCIETY)

WASHINGTON MEWS, CA. 1945

The Washington Mews initially provided access to the stables and the rear garden entrances leading to rowhouses along Washington Square, east of Fifth Avenue. In the 1930s, the rear gardens were replaced by miniature houses designed to complement the former stables facing them across the alley. (NATIONAL ARCHIVES)

PERMANENT WASHINGTON ARCH, 1932

This photograph shows a reenactment of George Washington's inauguration parade proceeding north from Washington Square Park. The park was once a gallows field, then a "potter's field," a burial ground for the poor. The NEW YORK AS IT IS IN 1833 AND CITIZENS' ADVERTISING DIRECTORY described the park as "the first of the series of open squares laid out within the last seven years in the upper part of the City. . . . During the present year, a range of superb private residences has been erected on the north side of the square and the name of the street, on the petition of the owners of those buildings, changed from Sixth Street to Waverly Place in honor of Sir Walter Scott." (EVERETT COLLECTION)

UPSTAIRS AT THE GARRET COFFEE HOUSE, 1917

Greenwich Village was a middle-class neighborhood until the turn of the century, when residences were subdivided into lodging hotels. By the beginning of World War I, the Village was a notorious bohemian district. The coffee houses of the nineteenth century were revived to great success among the locals and visiting "slummers" searching for life experiences in the Village, spending late hours in saloons and cafés drinking, smoking, and indulging in so-called "free-love." Its residents included a generation of artists, writers, social workers, and reformers who exposed political and social corruption in America. (JESSIE TARBOX BEALS/COLLECTION OF THE NEW-YORK HISTORICAL SOCIETY)

MAD HATTER TEA ROOM, CA. 1920

Jessie Tarbox Beals was a former teacher who taught herself photography and became the first woman press photographer. Some of the favorite meeting places of "true" Villagers were the Mad Hatter, Polly Holliday's, the Samovar, and the Purple Pub. Eliza Helen Criswall (pictured), otherwise known as Jimmie, ran the Mad Hatter. (JESSIE TARBOX BEALS/MUSEUM OF THE CITY OF NEW YORK)

JEFFERSON MARKET COURTHOUSE, CA. 1935

The Jefferson Market was established in 1833 as the central market for Greenwich Village. Fifty years later, the imposing Jefferson Market Courthouse with its red-brick clock tower was completed at Sixth Avenue and West 10th Street. To the far left is the corner of the Women's House of Detention that replaced the picturesque Jefferson Market in 1929. The Sixth Avenue "El" was raised in front of the market and courthouse in 1878, and stayed until it was removed in 1939. (BERENICE ABBOTT/MUSEUM OF THE CITY OF NEW YORK)

GANSEVOORT MARKET, CA. 1900

The Farmers Market was located in an abandoned train yard on the waterfront between Gansevoort and Little West 12th Street beginning in 1882. Farmers ferried their produce over from Long Island, Staten Island, and New Jersey to sell from 4 to 10 A.M. The market stayed remarkably the same over the decades. "Farmers in overalls and mud-caked shoes stand in carts, shouting their wares," described THE WPA GUIDE TO NYC in 1939. "Commission merchants, pushcart vendors, and restaurant buyers trudge warily from one stand to another, digging arms into baskets of fruits or vegetables to ascertain quality. Carts move continually in and out among the piled crates of tomatoes, beans, cabbages, lettuce, and other greens in the street." (COLLECTION OF THE NEW-YORK HISTORICAL SOCIETY)

CHELSEA PIERS #55–61, CA. 1905

The Hudson River piers were home to the world's greatest ocean liners, with the luxury ships QUEEN MARY, NORMANDIE, and EUROPA regularly docking there. For decades the White Star Line owned the transatlantic docks on West Street, Piers 55–61. (GEORGE P. HALL & SON/COLLECTION OF THE NEW-YORK HISTORICAL SOCIETY)

MEAT MARKET, CA. 1932

While most of the city slept, men were busy at work in the markets. The dark streets were always full of carts and trucks passing the food from jobbers to wholesalers and retailers, who supplied the city residents. (SOL LIBSOHN/NATIONAL ARCHIVES)

SUFFRAGETTES DEMONSTRATING
In the newly industrialized society of the nineteenth century, women lacked many of the civil and property rights enjoyed by men. Some women protested for suffrage, the right to vote for public officials and proposed legislation. Among the early suffragettes were college students who came to New York City from Vassar and Smith to demonstrate on behalf of all women. The suffragists gave birth to the Women's Liberation Movement of the later twentieth century. (EVERETT COLLECTION)

RED EMMA, CA. 1915
New Yorkers stood on soapboxes in Union Square to appeal to the masses. Emma Goldman supported the concerns of the Socialist Party and in 1906 founded MOTHER EARTH, a journal of radical political and cultural articles. Many saw her as the embodiment of anarchist idealism, and in 1919 she was deported to the Soviet Union for criticizing the military draft and the entry of the United States into World War I, and espousing other radical causes. (ARCHIVE PHOTOS)

MAY DAY IN UNION SQUARE, 1937

As Broadway cuts diagonally across much of Manhattan, it intersects the larger cross streets at 14th, 23rd, 34th, and 42nd Streets, creating squares. These squares became prime business locations. Union Square at Broadway and 14th Street was established as a park in 1809. The fashionable square was home to Steinway Hall and Tiffany's in 1860. Union Square gained the reputation for being the meeting place for dissidents and radicals, starting with the anti-draft riots in the 1860s. In this photograph, 35,000 of the city's left-wing labor forces stage a demonstration, marching past a reviewing stand. (EVERETT COLLECTION)

UNION SQUARE NAVY RECRUITING STATION, 1917–18

This replica of a U.S. battleship reminded New Yorkers of the dangers of living in a major port city during the war. A steel net was sunk and stretched across the Narrows to keep U-boats from sneaking into the Upper Bay. Over one and a half million American volunteers were recruited for World War I at stations such as these. (W. J. ROEGE/COLLECTION OF THE NEW-YORK HISTORICAL SOCIETY)

SALE OF LIBERTY BONDS IN UNION SQUARE, 1917

This replica of a submarine was placed in Union Square to promote the sale of war bonds. Raising money by war bonds was critical during World War I. (ROBERT L. BRACKLOW/COLLECTION OF THE NEW-YORK HISTORICAL SOCIETY)

MIDTO

W N

MIDTOWN IN THE MIST (ARCHIVE PHOTOS)

The Midtown district was first developed during the first half of the nineteenth century, along the waterfront, where factories and foundries were constructed close to water transportation. Warehouses and markets also fringed the wharves. On the West Side, Chelsea grew up around the quadrangle of the General Theological Seminary and became a small college town near the ferry lines to New Jersey. The East Side was known as the "gashouse" district, where enormous tanks stored the gas that was piped throughout the city to provide light. Above 42nd Street was predominantly rural. The city was forced to ban daytime cattle drives south of 34th Street in 1850.

But New York City was marching uptown from Lower Manhattan as business continued to boom downtown. Fifth Avenue was the pillar of Midtown and the showplace of New York. At first it was residential, with all the commerce located in Lower Manhattan. As the business center of the city crept ever northward, commerce invaded the residential splendor of Midtown. The grand homes were gradually replaced with large stores. By the turn of the century, both Fifth and Sixth Avenues between 14th and 23rd Street were lined with dry goods houses. This area was known as the "Ladies' Mile."

When the stores moved north to 34th Street, it became Manhattan's best-known shopping district. By World War I, Fifth Avenue was one of the most expensive streets in the world in terms of the goods sold and the property values. The avenue catered exclusively to wealthy "carriage trade" customers until the 1930s, when medium- and low-priced stores gradually appeared. But still Fifth Avenue retained its distinguished reputation for glamour and extravagance.

To provide access to the booming Midtown area, transportation hubs were established at Grand Central Station in 1871 and Pennsylvania Station in 1911. The theater district also moved north, settling in Times Square, and it came to be known as the Great White Way.

THE METROPOLITAN TOWER AND THE FLATIRON BUILDING, 1909.
This photograph of Madison Square is looking south at the junction of Fifth Avenue and Broadway. The Metropolitan Tower on the left was completed in 1908; with 50 stories it was the tallest in New York. On the right is the narrow Flatiron Building. These two skyscrapers reveal the remarkable leap in technology that took place at this time. At 20 stories high, the Flatiron was the tallest structure in the city in 1902. Its unprecedented height created unusual winds that often blew women's skirts above their ankles. Policemen used to shoo loungers away from the 23rd Street corner, creating the expression "23 skidoo." (MUSEUM OF THE CITY OF NEW YORK)

MADISON SQUARE, LOOKING NORTH, CA. 1906

The area of Madison Square started out as an arsenal, parade ground, and potter's field. In the early nineteenth century, the members of the New York Knickerbocker Baseball Club regularly gathered in the playing field at 27th Street and Madison Avenue. But the completion of the Flatiron Building in 1902 marked the end of the era of Madison Square as a social center. Within the next ten years, the area had become a commercial center. (MUSEUM OF THE CITY OF NEW YORK)

MADISON SQUARE PARK, 1898

Madison Square was a well-to-do neighborhood of neat
brownstone houses. Madison Square Park, opened in 1847,
was where mothers and nurses took their babies for a daily
stroll. (THE BYRON COLLECTION/MUSEUM OF THE CITY OF NEW YORK)

LADY LIBERTY'S EARLY HOME, LOOKING
NORTH FROM 23RD STREET, CA. 1880

In the background on the right in Madison Square Park rises
the torch of the Statue of Liberty, placed temporarily in the
park to help raise money needed to complete the structure.
Americans were accustomed to public statuary the size of the
Worth Monument obelisk (at left) and were overwhelmed by
the proposed size of France's gift to the United States.
(COLLECTION OF THE NEW-YORK HISTORICAL SOCIETY)

EDISON COMPANY DISPLAY, 1906
Thomas Edison's exhibition in Madison Square Garden of the products offered by his company. (ARCHIVE PHOTOS)

MADISON SQUARE GARDEN, 1903
The first Madison Square Garden, opened in 1879 at 26th Street, was torn down in 1889. It was replaced by this Moorish-style building—graced by colonnades at the ground and roof level—and remained here until 1925. It was designed by the prominent society architect Stanford White, who had a studio in the tall tower and was killed in the roof garden in 1906 by Harry K. Thaw, jealous husband of the showgirl Evelyn Nesbit. (IRVING UNDERHILL/MUSEUM OF THE CITY OF NEW YORK)

MADISON SQUARE PARK, CA. 1921
New Yorkers crowd into Madison Square Park to hear a radio broadcast of President Harding's address at the Tomb of the Unknown Soldier in Arlington, Virginia. (MORRIS ROSENFIELD/ MUSEUM OF THE CITY OF NEW YORK)

SPORTSMANS
SHOW

MADISON SQUARE GARDEN.
COPYRIGHT 1903 BY.

MARK TWAIN AT DELMONICO'S, 1905

One of New York's most famous restaurants was Delmonico's. Delmonico's was open to the general public but the restaurant was best known for its elaborate private dinners. Originally located downtown near Bowling Green, it moved to 14th Street in 1861 and stayed there until 1876, when it relocated to the north side of Madison Square, at 26th Street. Mark Twain's 70th birthday was celebrated at Delmonico's by more than 150 "literati," hosted by George Harvey, president of Harper & Brothers. Joseph Byron's photographs of the event were published in a special supplement to HARPER'S WEEKLY. At the time, Twain was living on Ninth Street and was part of the intellectual clique in Greenwich Village. (THE BYRON COLLECTION/MUSEUM OF THE CITY OF NEW YORK)

DIAMOND JIM BRADY AT DELMONICO'S

Delmonico's was frequented by everyone from the Vanderbilt family to Boss Tweed. Diamond Jim Brady, the portly man in front of the table, was an American businessman and philanthropist who began his career as a bellboy for the New York Central Railroad. As his wealth increased, so did his generosity and his penchant for the good life. He gave sizable loans and gifts, and he invested much of his fortune in jewelry, mostly diamonds, earning him his nickname. He was a legendary figure in New York City for his insatiable capacity for food, an appetite that he freely indulged at grand feasts. His friendship with singer Lillian Russell was a favorite gossip item. (WHITE STUDIO/MUSEUM OF THE CITY OF NEW YORK)

THE WALDORF-ASTORIA HOTEL, FIFTH AVENUE AND 33RD STREET, 1893

The Waldorf-Astoria Hotel resulted from a rivalry between two branches of the Astor family over the block of land they owned at 34th Street and Fifth Avenue. William Waldorf Astor built his lavish Waldorf Hotel in 1893, right next door to the home of his aunt, "The Mrs. Astor," whom he envied for her social success. Mrs. Astor soon moved north on Fifth Avenue, and on the vacated site her son, John Jacob IV, built an even more lavish hotel complete with turrets and elaborate finials—the Astoria. The two establishments were joined together in 1897 to form the largest hotel in the world, the Waldorf-Astoria Hotel, with nearly 1,300 rooms. (MUSEUM OF THE CITY OF NEW YORK)

J. P. MORGAN RESIDENCE, CA. 1915

The leisurely elegance of Murray Hill provided the atmosphere of affluence
sought by many of New York's "Four Hundred," the wealthiest families in the
city. J. P. Morgan commissioned this large brownstone mansion, designed with
subtle French Renaissance accents, to be built at 37th Street and Madison
Avenue. The Pierpont Morgan Library is the low white marble structure seen in
the background, which was designed later, in neoclassical style. The library
contained his valuable collection of sculpture, paintings, prints, objets d'art, rare
manuscripts, and books; it became a public library in 1924. (COLLECTION OF THE
NEW-YORK HISTORICAL SOCIETY)

THE WALDORF-ASTORIA HOTEL, 1931

The Waldorf-Astoria Hotel was relocated to 50th Street and Park Avenue.
The new art deco hotel opened in 1931, the same year as the Empire State
Building. The new Waldorf-Astoria was the last word in modernity, though it
retained traditionally beloved features such as Peacock Alley, the Astor Gallery,
and the Empire Room. In this photograph looking south, the spire of the
Chrysler Building rises in the background; in the foreground is St. Bartholomew's
Church. (EVERETT COLLECTION)

EMPIRE STATE BUILDING, 1938

The Empire State Building at 34th Street and Fifth Avenue was the tallest building in the world in 1931. The steel and limestone structure can hold more than 80,000 people, with 2,158,000 square feet of rentable floor space. Yet nearly one-third of the interior space consists of elevators and utilities. The appearance of the building was unusual for the time—the windows are set flush, making each tower wall appear to be one continuous sheet. (EVERETT COLLECTION)

WORKMEN CHISELING ATOP THE EMPIRE STATE BUILDING, 1930

The 102-story Empire State Building was erected remarkably fast, rising an average of four and a half stories every week. It was completed in one year and 45 days. The 200-foot dirigible mast on top enabled the structure to edge out the just-completed Chrysler Building (1930) for the world's tallest building. The mooring mast was used successfully only once, because dirigibles had trouble navigating in the high winds around the skyscraper. (IRVING BROWNING/COLLECTION OF THE NEW-YORK HISTORICAL SOCIETY)

AIRPLANE CRASHES INTO THE EMPIRE STATE BUILDING, 1945
An Army B-25 bomber, confused by heavy fog, crashed into the 79th floor of the Empire State Building. Fourteen people
were killed but only minimal damage was done to the structure. The pilot didn't see the skyscraper because of a wartime
dim-out ordered for the city by officials who feared that the bright lights reflecting on the sky created a target for enemy
planes. (EVERETT COLLECTION)

EMPIRE STATE BUILDING AT NIGHT, CA. 1930
Despite the economic depression that gripped the country, construction on the Empire State Building began in 1930 and
was completed in 1931. This night photograph shows the skyscraper as historian Will Durant described it before the
Second World War: "The Empire State Building is as sublime as Chartres Cathedral." (IRVING BROWNING/COLLECTION OF THE
NEW-YORK HISTORICAL SOCIETY)

SUBWAY CAVE-IN, 1915

An accidental explosion of dynamite during the construction of the subway turned Seventh Avenue from 23rd to 25th Street into a 30-foot chasm. The wooden planking that had once covered the street collapsed into the subway trench. A streetcar was buried, killing and injuring many people. The street was repaired and the Seventh Avenue subway was eventually completed. (FREDERICK HUGH SMYTH/COLLECTION OF THE NEW-YORK HISTORICAL SOCIETY)

WALLPAPER FACTORY FIRE AT 34TH STREET, CA. 1910

Factory fires were not uncommon. Sweeping changes in New York's fire-safety codes were prompted by the terrible fire at the Triangle Shirtwaist Company factory in 1911 that killed 146 workers, all of them women. The disaster also lent impetus to the American labor movement in its goal to protect workers and improve safety on the job. (FREDERICK H. SMYTH/COLLECTION OF THE NEW-YORK HISTORICAL SOCIETY)

BUILDING PENNSYLVANIA STATION, FROM SEVENTH AVENUE AND 31ST STREET

"With the advent of the Pennsylvania's big station and tunnel in the heart of the old Tenderloin, that famous center of vice and blackmail passes into history," reported the NEW YORK HERALD in 1903. In all, 500 buildings were torn down so Pennsylvania Station could be built from 31st to 33rd Street between Seventh and Eighth Avenues. The Pennsylvania Railroad tunneled under both rivers to connect Manhattan with New Jersey and Long Island. The station was completed in 1911, creating the only continuous rail line from New England to the Southern states. (BROWN BROTHERS/MUSEUM OF THE CITY OF NEW YORK)

INTERIOR OF PENNSYLVANIA STATION

The station was designed by McKim, Mead, and White along Roman classical lines, and was considered to be a monument of modern architecture. The ticket area duplicated the Tepidarium, the baths of Rome built by Emperor Caracalla in the years 212–235 A.D. The vast waiting room was a concourse with 150-foot vaulting arches of latticework wrought iron and glass. The terminal reached its zenith of activity in the 1940s when a train arrived or departed every 46 seconds. (EDWIN LEVICK/ARCHIVE PHOTOS)

EDWIN LEVICK
NEW YORK

EXIT

Nᵒ6171 Penna R. R. Station
Copyright 1911 by
Geo. P. Hall & Son, New York.

WAITING REDCAPS AT PENNSYLVANIA STATION, 1938

Redcaps wait for cabs under the classic facade of the world's largest railroad station. Access streets running through the building enabled passengers and baggage to be let off or picked up with a minimum of interference with traffic. The redcaps offered travelers assistance with their luggage and directions to the proper track, ensuring that Pennsylvania Station was one of the finest terminals in the world. (COLLECTION OF HOWARD FRANK)

THE CONCOURSE OF PENNSYLVANIA STATION, 1911

This photograph was taken in the early morning when the station was nearly empty, capturing the sheer architectural beauty of the glass-roofed concourse over the track platforms. (GEORGE P. HALL & SON/MUSEUM OF THE CITY OF NEW YORK)

FOUR OF THE WORLD'S LARGEST LINERS HELD FOR ARMS INSPECTION, 1939

This photograph was taken as World War II hovered over the four countries that owned the largest ocean liners. From bottom to top are the North German Lloyd Liner the BREMEN, the French Liner the NORMANDIE, the British Cunard Liner the ACQUITANIA, and the Italian Liner the ROMA. These ships were held for inspection by U.S. Customs officials who refused to release clearance papers until the ships had been searched for "implements of war." When the foreign governments protested, President Roosevelt argued that the United States would be liable if the vessels were armed and damaged other ships at sea. (EVERETT COLLECTION)

ARRIVAL OF THE SS QUEEN MARY, SEPTEMBER 1939

This photograph was taken on the pier after the arrival of the QUEEN MARY from war-torn Europe. The record-breaking passenger list totaled 2,331 people, with more than 200 forced to sleep on cots in the public rooms during the Atlantic passage. The QUEEN MARY also carried $44,550,000 in gold on this passage. During World War II, the luxury liner trade came to a halt due to the hostilities on the seas. Many liners, including the QUEEN MARY, were commandeered by their countries of ownership and used as hospital or troop ships. (EVERETT COLLECTION)

THE BATTLESHIP KANSAS, IN NEW YORK HARBOR, CA. 1900

The battleship was the flagship in the world's navies from the Civil War to World War II, when the aircraft carrier was introduced. The KANSAS was one of the first true battleships, authorized by Congress for the U.S. Navy in 1890. This classic example of the ironclad fighting ship was one of a series named for states: the INDIANA, the MASSACHUSETTS, and the OREGON, among others. (ROBERT L. BRACKLOW/COLLECTION OF THE NEW-YORK HISTORICAL SOCIETY)

SAILOR GETTING HIS SHOES SHINED, 1944

New York City was a main port for the movement of troops and the shipment of cargo during war. Sailors enjoyed being on leave in New York. (MUSEUM OF THE CITY OF NEW YORK)

CONSTRUCTION OF THE NEW YORK TIMES BUILDING, CA. 1900

THE NEW YORK TIMES daily newspaper was founded in 1851, and purchased in 1896 by Adolph S. Ochs. Ochs turned it into one of the greatest newspapers in the world through his dedication to report the news accurately and avoid editorial bias—"All the News That's Fit to Print." In 1902, architects Eidlitz and MacKenzie built the 25-story New York Times Building, cunningly designed to fit on a triangular plot of land in what then became known as Times Square. Ochs instituted the annual New Year's Eve ball-dropping extravaganza with the opening of the new building. (ROBERT L. BRACKLOW/COLLECTION OF THE NEW-YORK HISTORICAL SOCIETY)

TIMES SQUARE, LOOKING SOUTH, 1923

Times Square, where 42nd Street meets Seventh Avenue and Broadway, was known as the "Crossroads of the World." By the turn of the century, theaters had followed Broadway north to Times Square, which has been the heart of New York's theater district ever since. (W. J. ROEGE/COLLECTION OF THE NEW-YORK HISTORICAL SOCIETY)

SNOW FALLING IN TIMES SQUARE, 1935

This photograph, looking north from 46th Street, shows incandescent billboards as they appeared behind a curtain of swirling snow during a winter storm. Times Square was so famous for its illuminated signs that it was nicknamed the "Great White Way" by O. J. Gude, an advertising man at the turn of the century. The brilliant billboards and theater marquees competed for attention with numerous hotels and restaurants in the area, all serving the visitors—as many as 100,000—who came to New York City every night. (EVERETT COLLECTION)

42ND STREET BILLBOARDS, CA. 1900

The blizzard of billboards in Times Square was sanctioned by New York City statute. In 1921, Englishman G. K. Chesterton described the signs as "advertising everything from pork to pianos." (ROBERT L. BRACKLOW/COLLECTION OF THE NEW-YORK HISTORICAL SOCIETY)

TIMES SQUARE ON NEW YEAR'S EVE, JANUARY 1, 1940
Huge crowds jam every corner of Times Square with festive good cheer to celebrate New Year's Eve. Waiting for the ball to drop at the stroke
of midnight had become an annual affair. (EVERETT COLLECTION)

CENTRAL THEATER, BROADWAY AND 47TH STREET, CA. 1930 (above)
Crowds gathered on Broadway during the opening week of the movie ALL QUIET ON THE WESTERN FRONT. (IRVING BROWNING/COLLECTION OF THE NEW-YORK HISTORICAL SOCIETY)

STARS IN NEW YORK CITY (facing)
Clockwise from top left: producer, songwriter, and performer George M. Cohan ("Give My Regards to Broadway") hails a cab for Tallulah Bankhead; actor John Barrymore and his wife, Patricia Waters; "America's Sweetheart," Mary Pickford and her husband, Douglas Fairbanks; actors Lynn Fontanne and Alfred Lunt at a dress rehearsal of THE PIRATE, 1942. (ARCHIVE PHOTOS)

INSIDE THE LATIN QUARTER NIGHTCLUB, TIMES SQUARE, CA. 1945 (left)

"It was the district of glorified dancing girls and millionaire playboys," reported THE WPA GUIDE TO NYC of Times Square, "and, on a different plane, of dime-a-dance hostesses and pleasure-seeking clerks. Here, too, in a permanent moralizing tableau, appear the extremes of success and failure characteristic of Broadway's spectacular professions: gangsters and racketeers, panhandlers and derelicts, youthful stage stars and aging burlesque comedians, world heavyweight champions and once-acclaimed beggars." (ARCHIVE PHOTOS)

EL MOROCCO, CA. 1930 (above)
A belt of nightclubs stretched up Times Square and across Midtown to the East Side. (ARCHIVE PHOTOS)

LUCKY LUCIANO, CA. 1945 (right)
Charles "Lucky" Luciano (shown under arrest, on right in photo) was a Sicilian-born racketeer who controlled prostitution and narcotics, becoming one of the most powerful people in American organized crime in the 1930s. Luciano remained a major influence even after his deportation to Italy in 1946. (ARCHIVE PHOTOS)

SALON DES ARTS, 52ND STREET, CA. 1930 (facing, below)
Burlesque houses were a long-standing tradition in New York theater. By 1869, theaters in the city were offering "naked drama," which meant the women wore tights giving the illusion of nudity. (IRVING BROWNING/COLLECTION OF THE NEW-YORK HISTORICAL SOCIETY)

ROTHMAN'S PAWNSHOP ON EIGHTH AVENUE, 1938

The first pawnshop opened in New York City in 1822. Customers exchanged household goods, clothing, jewelry, or personal effects for money and agreed to repay the amount plus interest in order to get their collateral back. Also known as hockshops, these businesses were typically established in districts where money was in short supply. (BERENICE ABBOTT/MUSEUM OF THE CITY OF NEW YORK)

MADISON SQUARE GARDEN, 1937

In 1925, Madison Square Garden was moved from the building in Madison Square to West 50th Street and Eighth Avenue. The new Garden had a large arena suitable for boxing and team sporting events and a seating capacity of nearly 19,000 people. In this photograph, legionnaires are marching inside for the opening session of their national convention. (EVERETT COLLECTION)

RADIO CITY MUSIC HALL, 1937
Designed by Donald Deskey in the art deco style, Radio City Music Hall was opened in 1932. From Georgia O'Keeffe's flower murals in the ladies room to the gold leaf ceiling in the lobby, the interior decoration of the Music Hall was the finest money could buy. (ARCHIVE PHOTOS)

THE ROCKETTES
Radio City Music Hall was superlative in every way. At the time, it was the largest indoor theater ever built, with both the orchestra and the movie screen bigger than any other in the world. It ran both motion pictures and variety shows featuring the famous Rockettes, considered to be the world's finest precision dancers. (ARCHIVE PHOTOS)

LAYING THE CORNERSTONE OF CARNEGIE HALL, 1889

Louise Whitfield Carnegie, silver trowel in hand, presided over the laying of the cornerstone of Carnegie Hall at 57th Street and Seventh
Avenue. Her husband, Andrew Carnegie, is standing to the left of the man in the apron and top hat (his face is partly obscured by ropes).
Mrs. Carnegie was a devoted amateur classical musician who helped persuade her husband to fund the new concert hall. (ARCHIVE PHOTOS)

ROCKEFELLER CENTER AT NIGHT

Two hundred buildings were torn down when Rockefeller Center was commenced in 1929. Construction of the vast 19-building complex from West 48th to 51st Street took ten years and employed 75,000 men. John D. Rockefeller, Jr., wanted to maximize the income he could get from the office space, but he also wanted it to be "as beautiful as possible." Although New York City buildings usually faced the street, Rockefeller Center structures were grouped around a vast central court. The 70-story Radio Corporation of America Building was the tallest in the complex. (ARCHIVE PHOTOS)

PROMETHEUS IN THE COURTYARD OF ROCKEFELLER PLAZA, CA. 1930

Sculptures, mosaics, wall murals, and wood-carved details were included in the original design of Rockefeller Plaza, created by Henry Hofmeister, H. W. Corbett, and Raymond Hood. The Plaza's central courtyard was flooded for ice-skating during the winter and served as an outdoor café in the summer. THE WPA GUIDE TO NYC raved over the newest addition to the city: "In its architecture Rockefeller Center stands as distinctly for New York as the Louvre stands for Paris." (IRVING BROWNING/COLLECTION OF THE NEW-YORK HISTORICAL SOCIETY)

CHRISTMAS TREE AT ROCKEFELLER CENTER

The tradition of raising a Christmas tree at Rockefeller Center dates back to 1931, while Rockefeller Center was still being constructed. A small tree was placed on the site of the British Empire Building and La Maison Française soon after the houses in that area were demolished. The formal Christmas tree display began in 1933 in front of the RCA Building. (ARCHIVE PHOTOS)

5TH AVE. LOOKING SOUTH FROM 42ND ST. - 1880 -

MANSION HOUSES, 1880

The "House of Mansions" was built in 1855 across from the Croton Reservoir at Fifth Avenue and 42nd Street. At the time, the eleven Gothic-style houses were too far uptown to appeal to society, so the residences were combined into one building to become the Rutgers Female College. (MUSEUM OF THE CITY OF NEW YORK)

THE CROTON RESERVOIR AT FIFTH AVENUE AND 42ND STREET, 1899

The city received its first dependable water supply when the Croton Aqueduct system opened in 1842. The massive Croton distributing reservoir in Midtown could hold 20 million gallons of water. The walls resembled an Egyptian temple, and they loomed over Fifth Avenue at 42nd Street. New Yorkers delighted in walking along the promenade on top, which provided an unparalleled view of the island. (ROBERT L. BRACKLOW/COLLECTION OF THE NEW-YORK HISTORICAL SOCIETY)

CRYSTAL PALACE, SIXTH AVENUE, 40TH TO 42ND STREETS, 1853

The huge cast-iron and glass Crystal Palace was built to house the first American world's fair in 1853–54, in what became Bryant Park behind the present-day New York Public Library. The theme of the fair was "Exhibition of the Industry of All Nations" and among the 4,000 exhibits from around the world were Singer sewing machines, a model of Morse's telegraph, new printing presses, and a remarkable device that made something called "drinking soda." Supposedly fireproof, the palace caught fire and collapsed five years after it was built. (COLLECTION OF THE NEW-YORK HISTORICAL SOCIETY)

AERIAL VIEW OF FIFTH AVENUE AND THE NEW YORK PUBLIC LIBRARY, CA. 1935

The city's shopping center relentlessly marched up Fifth Avenue in the late nineteenth century, from 14th Street to 42nd Street and beyond. This picture shows Fifth Avenue with the steps to the New York Public Library on the right. (IRVING BROWNING/COLLECTION OF THE NEW-YORK HISTORICAL SOCIETY)

THE NEW YORK PUBLIC LIBRARY, 1919

In 1895, three great book collections were donated to New York City—the Astor Library, the Lenox Library, and the Tilden Trust—and in 1899–1900 the Croton Reservoir was torn down to make way for the new library at Fifth Avenue and 42nd Street. The Beaux-Arts design by John M. Carrere and Thomas Hastings took over a decade to construct. It is still considered to be one of the greatest libraries in the world. In this photograph the library is decorated to celebrate the Allied victory in World War I. (THE BYRON COLLECTION/MUSEUM OF THE CITY OF NEW YORK)

LUNCH COUNTER
"New York City is truly the home of the quick lunch counters," reported the CATERER MONTHLY in 1898. "Nowhere else in the world will you find a class of business people whose average time taken for their midday meal is but 15 minutes." (SOL LIBSOHN/ NATIONAL ARCHIVES)

TEMPO OF THE CITY, 42ND STREET AT FIFTH AVENUE, 1938
Fifth Avenue was the height of sophistication, and it became the country's leading shopping avenue by World War I. (BERENICE ABBOTT/MUSEUM OF THE CITY OF NEW YORK)

SANDWICH BOARDS, CA.1929
Charles Dickens was the first to give the nickname "sandwich men" to those who sauntered through the streets wearing two advertising placards strapped together at the shoulders. (IRVING BROWNING/COLLECTION OF THE NEW-YORK HISTORICAL SOCIETY)

GARMENT DISTRICT, 1944
The garment business was New York City's top industry from the late nineteenth century until World War II. Begun on the Lower East Side, the "rag trade" followed the city's move north, marching up the streets between Sixth and Ninth Avenues, from 14th Street up to 34th Street. The curbs were lined with trucks, unloading materials and loading the finished products, while "push boys" rolled racks of garments through the congested streets. (MUSEUM OF THE CITY OF NEW YORK)

MACY'S ON HERALD SQUARE, CA. 1910

Macy's department store started out as a shop on Sixth Avenue and 14th Street. The retailer built the "world's largest department store" at 34th Street and Broadway in 1902, inaugurating Herald Square as Manhattan's main shopping district. The small five-story building in the corner belonged to merchants who refused to sell their tiny plot of land to Macy's. (COLLECTION OF THE NEW-YORK HISTORICAL SOCIETY)

LORD & TAYLOR'S ON BROADWAY

This is the first Lord & Taylor's, opened on Broadway at 20th Street in 1872. In 1914, Lord & Taylor's moved to 38th Street. (MUSEUM OF THE CITY OF NEW YORK)

SERVICEWOMEN WINDOW-SHOP AT SAKS FIFTH AVENUE, 1944

Saks Fifth Avenue at 50th Street was the first of the larger stores to be built on upper Fifth Avenue in 1924. Saks, along with Bergdorf-Goodman, Lord & Taylor, and Bonwit Teller, became widely known for their striking window displays, designed with the detail and care of a stage set for a Broadway musical. (MUSEUM OF THE CITY OF NEW YORK)

SALVATION ARMY, 1906

The Salvation Army was founded in England in 1878 as an international Christian charitable organization offering food and housing for the needy and spiritual salvation for the "fallen, degraded, and forsaken." It introduced the trademark donation kettle in 1891 with the slogan, "Keep the pot boiling." (THE BYRON COLLECTION/MUSEUM OF THE CITY OF NEW YORK)

MAGAZINE VENDOR, 1932

Periodicals became a popular way to get information in the 1920s and 30s. TIME was created in 1923, NEWSWEEK in 1933, and LIFE in 1936. Most of the early women's magazines, such as BETTER HOMES AND GARDENS, 1922, and FAMILY CIRCLE, 1932, catered to women at home, but VOGUE, founded in 1892, became increasingly popular in New York City because of its fashion pages. (IRVING BROWNING/ COLLECTION OF THE NEW-YORK HISTORICAL SOCIETY)

FIFTH AVENUE ON EASTER MORNING, 1889 (above, left)

New Yorkers considered St. Patrick's Cathedral, which resembled the Cologne Cathedral in France, to be one of the noblest structures in the city. As early as 1869, THE NEW YORK TIMES commented on the social nature of worship on Easter morning: "The day being so pleasant, the streets and parks were filled with pedestrians. . . . The ladies were out in full force, looking doubly charming under the influence of those genial skies." (NATIONAL ARCHIVES, PICTURES OF THE AMERICAN CITY)

WARTIME ST. PATRICK'S, 1941 (above, right)

The annual Easter Parade included worshippers from all the churches in the neighborhood of St. Patrick's, including St. Thomas and the Collegiate Church of St. Nicholas. Since the age of bonnets and bustles, thousands of sightseers traditionally gathered to watch the parade. But during World War II, the society watchers were replaced by a troubled and devout mass of worshippers who clogged the avenue outside St. Patrick's. (MUSEUM OF THE CITY OF NEW YORK)

THE EASTER PARADE, 1900 (facing)

Society flocked to Fifth Avenue to stroll up and down the sidewalks, while the street was filled with carriages and motor cars. THE NEW YORK TIMES may be responsible for naming the annual event in 1886, reporting that the avenue was a moving, living fashion plate: "It was altogether a brilliant picture . . . and country cousins who had come to see the Easter parade gazed lovingly and longingly at the costumes of such cunning fancies as their own village dressmaker never dreamed." (NATIONAL ARCHIVES, PICTURES OF THE AMERICAN CITY)

GRAND CENTRAL STATION, 1871

In 1869, Cornelius Vanderbilt broke ground on the first Grand Central Station, at 42nd Street. I. C. Buckhout designed the handsome Victorian station then known as Grand Central Depot. It remained the only railroad terminal in Manhattan until the early twentieth century. (COLLECTION OF THE NEW-YORK HISTORICAL SOCIETY)

GRAND CENTRAL STATION, LOOKING NORTH FROM 42ND STREET, CA. 1940

The second Grand Central Station opened in 1913 on the site of the first terminal. Its Beaux-Arts design, a marvel of modern efficiency by architects Warren, Wetmore, Reed, and Stem, included a traffic viaduct for Park Avenue to encircle the station. (COLLECTION OF THE NEW-YORK HISTORICAL SOCIETY)

INTERIOR OF GRAND CENTRAL STATION, CA. 1940

Grand Central Station was an architectural landmark with colossal interior space. The main concourse is 120 feet wide, 375 feet long, and has vaulted ceilings 125 feet high. By the 1930s, the number of people who passed through Grand Central every year approximated the total population of the United States. (COLLECTION OF THE NEW-YORK HISTORICAL SOCIETY)

MARGARET BOURKE-WHITE ON THE CHRYSLER BUILDING

Margaret Bourke-White was one of the innovators of the photo essay. Here she is photographing New York from atop a steel gargoyle on the Chrysler Building. Bourke-White began her career as an architectural photographer in 1927; she was one of the first four staff photographers for LIFE magazine, in 1936. When her transport ship was torpedoed and sunk in the Atlantic during World War II, she survived to become the first woman photographer attached to the U.S. armed forces. (OSCAR GRAUBNER/COURTESY OF THE MARGARET BOURKE-WHITE ESTATE/LIFE MAGAZINE © TIME INC.)

ROW OF TOWERS ON 42ND STREET, CA. 1932

Construction for these skyscrapers had begun during the 1920s and was being completed just as the Great Depression hit America. In the foreground, from the right, are the Daily News Building (1930), the Chrysler Building (1930), and the Chanin Building (1929). (IRVING BROWNING/COLLECTION OF THE NEW-YORK HISTORICAL SOCIETY)

EAST RIVER SHORELINE AT 53RD STREET, CA. 1859

On the Upper East Side, the shoreline was developed first. From 59th Street down to the Gashouse District near 14th Street, the waterfront was a series of isolated factories, tenements, small stores, shanties, and dumps. The East River Drive was built during World War II, covering the waterfront district with a wide highway from Lower Manhattan to Harlem. (MUSEUM OF THE CITY OF NEW YORK)

DUMPING SNOW INTO THE EAST RIVER

Starting in the 1920s, there were sporadic attempts to remove snow from the streets. Men shoveled drifts into dump trucks which deposited the snow in the river. These trucks, with their front spoke wheels and hard rubber tires, replaced the horse-drawn workcarts of the early twentieth century. (NATIONAL ARCHIVES)

YOULE'S SHOT TOWER AND 18TH-CENTURY HOUSE, CA. 1900

This photograph was taken of East 53rd Street 40 years after the photograph opposite. The tall tower manufactured shot ammunition. Molten lead was poured through sieves at the top of the 125-foot tower; while dropping, the lead formed balls that solidified near the bottom of their fall. The shot was collected in water and sorted for size and shape. (ROBERT L. BRACKLOW/COLLECTION OF THE NEW-YORK HISTORICAL SOCIETY)

UNEMPLOYED LIVING IN A SHANTYTOWN, 1933 (above)
This shantytown was erected during the Great Depression on 35th Street near the East River. One out of every four employable New Yorkers was jobless. (EVERETT COLLECTION)

BELLEVUE HOSPITAL, CA. 1873 (facing, above)
Many of the first structures built north of 14th Street were large public institutions such as Stewart's Home for Women on 32nd Street and the Old Men and Women's Hospital on Lenox Hill. Bellevue Hospital, formerly the old infirmary on the site of City Hall, was moved in 1816 to an almshouse on old Belle Vue Farm on 26th Street near the East River. Bellevue is the oldest general hospital on the North American continent. Bellevue Medical College opened in 1861, and a school of nursing was opened in 1873. (COLLECTION OF THE NEW-YORK HISTORICAL SOCIETY)

BLACKWELL'S ISLAND, 1908 (facing, below)
Now known as Roosevelt Island, the cigar-shaped East River island between Manhattan and Queens was called Blackwell's Island until 1921. The city bought the island in 1828 and built a workhouse, almshouse, hospitals, and a penitentiary there. Blackwell's was renamed Welfare Island when millions in tax dollars were spent on construction of great public health institutions there. Both New York State and New York City sent sick, elderly, poverty-stricken, and mentally unstable citizens to the vast complexes of homes and hospitals on the island. (MUSEUM OF THE CITY OF NEW YORK)

WELFARE ISLAND, 1939

The Queensboro Bridge, completed in 1909, spanned the river from Queens to Manhattan, using Blackwell's Island (later Welfare Island, then Roosevelt Island) as a foundation for two of its towers. The complex in front of the bridge is the Welfare Hospital for Chronic Diseases, then the most modern facility of its kind in the world, with a bed capacity of 1,600. The hospital was affiliated with the Columbia University College of Physicians and Surgeons, and the New York University College of Medicine. (EVERETT COLLECTION)

LOOKING AT MANHATTAN FROM THE QUEENSBORO BRIDGE, 1930

This photograph of the cantilever structure of the Queensboro Bridge appeared in ARCHITECTURAL FORUM, emphasizing the angular beauty of the bridge. The Queensboro Bridge is a remarkable 7,500 feet long. When the bridge opened in 1909, it ushered in a period of enormous growth in Queens; the population quadrupled over the next two decades to over one million people. (IRVING BROWNING/COLLECTION OF THE NEW-YORK HISTORICAL SOCIETY)

UPTOW

U ptown was decidedly rural until the late nineteenth century with small farms, breweries, lumberyards, and charity wards dotting the hills and marshes. There was a vast squatters' village in what would become Central Park, from which scavengers would venture into the city every day.

Fifth Avenue was a rutted country road above 59th Street; it wasn't graded until after the Civil War. But by the time Central Park was completed in 1876, the residential section of Fifth Avenue had moved north again, squeezed away from the invading commerce in Midtown. Wealthy New Yorkers bought land along the east side of Fifth Avenue and constructed grand limestone mansions facing Central Park. This strip soon became known as "Millionaires' Row."

The transformation of 843 acres in the middle of Manhattan into Central Park was a singular achievement, creating a world hidden from the city where generations of New Yorkers would enjoy year-round escape from their hectic lives.

The Upper West Side stayed under cultivation or consisted of small country estates until the Ninth Avenue "El" (elevated railroad) opened the area for development when it was extended up the West Side in 1879. As late as the 1890s, bicycle riders often biked up beautiful Bloomingdale Road, which later became an extension of Broadway.

Uptown Manhattan was invigorated by the construction of the Cathedral of St. John the Divine beginning in the 1880s, as well as Columbia College and St. Luke's Hospital.

A large section of northern Manhattan was named for the Holland town of Harlem by the Dutch Governor Peter Stuyvesant. Stuyvesant developed the section "for the promotion of agriculture and as a place of amusement for the citizens of New Amsterdam."

In the late nineteenth century, Harlem became a haven for clerks, small merchants, newly married couples, and professionals with families. Harlem had its share of fine residences, wealthy churches, theaters, hotels, and cafés, but it also had an area of tenements and brick flats where poor Jews, African-Americans, Italians, and Latinos lived.

Roi Ottley points out in INSIDE BLACK AMERICA, "Actually Harlem did not begin to take shape and character as a Negro community until 1910." By World War I, the city's black population had jumped to 150,000, drawn to the city for the boom-time pay. A decade later, twice as many African-Americans faced the lean times of the Great Depression. Throughout, however, black Harlem left an indelible mark on American culture, most notably through its cosmopolitan culture and nightlife, and especially the innovative music called jazz.

THE PLAZA HOTEL ON FIFTH AVENUE, 1939
The Grand Army Plaza at the southeast corner of Central Park was surrounded by stately hotels in the early twentieth century. The Renaissance-style Plaza Hotel had a special cachet because it was set back from Fifth Avenue on its own piazza with a picturesque fountain. Opened in 1907, the expensive suites each consisted of a parlor, bedroom, and bath for $12–20 a day. The distinguished guests enthused at the view over Central Park, which the NEW YORK HERALD claimed rivaled "an outlook from the Alps."
(H. L. WITTEMAN/COLLECTION OF THE NEW-YORK HISTORICAL SOCIETY)

MADISON AVENUE LOOKING NORTH,
CA. 1870
From 55th Street north, the grid-lines of the city plan stand out in stark relief in the gouged earth. Never have the rich and the poor rubbed elbows so closely as on the Upper East Side. When Andrew Carnegie built his mansion at 91st Street and Fifth Avenue in 1905, his nearest neighbor lived in a shanty. (THE J. CLARENCE DAVIES COLLECTION/MUSEUM OF THE CITY OF NEW YORK)

MADISON AVENUE, 1945
After World War I, Madison Avenue was rapidly transformed into one of the world's most costly commerce strips. These shops supplied luxury and imported items to the upper-class neighborhood: antiques, luggage, flowers, paintings, perfume, gifts, pet supplies, and expensive garments and furs.
(COLLECTION OF THE NEW-YORK HISTORICAL SOCIETY)

VIENNA BAKERY, 1899

Yorkville was known as the German section of the city, but Czechs, Slovaks, Hungarians, and Irish also lived east of Lexington Avenue between 59th and 90th Streets. This bakery is on Third Avenue, the old Boston Post Road. (COLLECTION OF THE NEW-YORK HISTORICAL SOCIETY)

GRAND CENTRAL TERMINAL RAIL YARDS, FROM PARK AVENUE AT 50TH STREET, 1905
The large train shed was built directly behind the original Grand Central Station. Beyond that was the double-deck railroad yard with 41 tracks on the upper level and 26 on the lower level. When the new Grand Central terminal was built in 1913, Park Avenue covered the yard tracks, which converged into the main tracks that ran below ground until 96th Street. (COLLECTION OF THE NEW-YORK HISTORICAL SOCIETY)

PARK AVENUE, LOOKING SOUTH FROM THE NORTHWEST CORNER OF 61ST STREET, 1924
After World War I, architects developed a way to construct skyscraper apartments on stilts, freeing them from the vibrations of the tracks below. Park Avenue, built over the railroad yards, quickly became fashionable. It is one of the broadest thoroughfares in the city, with a well-tended narrow park running down the center. The exteriors of the apartment buildings were uniformly bland, but each apartment offered the most modern of conveniences along with ample light and air. (THE BYRON COLLECTION/MUSEUM OF THE CITY OF NEW YORK)

THE VANDERBILT HOUSE ON FIFTH AVENUE AND 58TH LOOKING SOUTH (above)
The Vanderbilt family owned no less than half a dozen elegant mansions on Fifth Avenue. "Finest of all are the Vanderbilt palaces," praised Hans Knickerbocker in 1889. "The Vanderbilts have come nobly forward and shown the world how millionaires ought to live." (ROBERT L. BRACKLOW/ MUSEUM OF THE CITY OF NEW YORK)

THE ASTOR MANSION AT FIFTH AVENUE AND 65TH STREET, 1905 (facing, above)
The Astor family had long owned a country estate on the Upper East Side, and they were among the first to purchase land on Fifth Avenue across from Central Park. This photograph of the Astor Mansion on East 65th Street includes other modern castles built by captains of industry. The NEW YORK HERALD described Fifth Avenue in 1898 as "a solid mile and a half of millionaires' residences, practically without a break, except where a vacant spot awaits the coming of still another Croesus." (MUSEUM OF THE CITY OF NEW YORK)

TEMPLE BETH-EL, 1901 (facing, below)
The imposing Temple Beth-El, designed by William Arnold Brunner and Thomas Tryon, towered over Fifth Avenue at East 76th Street. On the morning of the dedication in 1891, the NEW YORK DAILY TRIBUNE described the temple as "massive and striking in its architectural beauty . . . with an immense central structure, half dome, half tower, 51 feet in diameter at the base and rising to a height of 140 feet . . . flanked by two smaller towers built of iron and covered with copper, with tracery of gilded copper." (THE BYRON COLLECTION/MUSEUM OF THE CITY OF NEW YORK)

METROPOLITAN MUSEUM OF ART (above)

Considered to have one of the best art collections in the world, the museum was formed in 1870 by members of the Union League Club. Both the zoo and the Metropolitan Museum of Art were not in the original plans of Central Park, but park designer Frederick Law Olmsted agreed that they served public recreation. Calvert Vaux and Jacob Wrey Mould designed the original red-brick museum building in neo-Gothic style. A white facade was built on Fifth Avenue; wings added in 1910 and 1926 vastly extended the exhibit space. (WURTS BROTHERS COLLECTION/MUSEUM OF THE CITY OF NEW YORK)

STEREOGRAPH OF CONSTRUCTION IN CENTRAL PARK (facing, above left)

Central Park was approved by the state legislature in 1853. A committee awarded the $2,000 prize money for the winning design to Frederick Law Olmsted and Calvert Vaux. Their Greensward plan created a pastoral landscape in the English Romantic tradition, transforming 843 acres in the middle of Manhattan island into a lush park. (ARCHIVE PHOTOS)

THE OBELISK IN CENTRAL PARK, CA. 1900 (facing, above right)

The obelisk was commonly known as Cleopatra's Needle even though it was never associated with the last Egyptian queen. It was given to New York in 1880 by the khedive of Egypt, and was transported with great difficulty from the East River to the park. For months the structure was rolled inch by inch on cannonballs until it reached its pedestal behind the Metropolitan Museum of Art. (ROBERT L. BRACKLOW/COLLECTION OF THE NEW-YORK HISTORICAL SOCIETY)

BETHESDA FOUNTAIN FROM THE TERRACE, 1894 (facing, below)

The only statue included in Olmsted and Vaux's original plan was at Bethesda Fountain. The stairways and arcade of the terrace were designed to complement the central fountain featuring the statue. (J. S. JOHNSTON/COLLECTION OF THE NEW-YORK HISTORICAL SOCIETY)

GORILLA AT THE CENTRAL PARK ZOO, 1944
A large holiday crowd gathers on the Fourth of July to watch the antics of a gorilla in the zoo. The Zoological Garden was established in the late 1860s, with nearly 800 species housed in the old Arsenal Building. In 1934, a new brick complex was built on Fifth Avenue at 65th Street and was renamed the Central Park Zoo. (EVERETT COLLECTION)

LIMITED EXPRESS, CA. 1904
Numerous areas in Central Park were set aside for children. In the gaslight era, they could ride in rented barouches drawn by teams of goats down the long mall. Children could also ride the carousel, splash in the wading pools, and climb on fanciful statues like ALICE IN WONDERLAND. There was free music at the band shell, carefully leveled walkways for bicycle and roller skating, and a miniature steam-engine train called the Limited Express. (ARCHIVE PHOTOS)

BOAT LANDING·CENTRAL PARK.

THE OLD BOATHOUSE, CA. 1900

This airy, rustic boathouse replaced the original boathouse built in 1873. The Board of Commissioners licensed two classes of boats—small private rowboats and the passage or omnibus variety, which cost ten cents for a two-mile round-trip journey. The meandering lake offered secluded bays and nooks far away from the bustle of the city for New Yorkers who wanted to relax. (MUSEUM OF THE CITY OF NEW YORK)

SHANTYTOWN ON THE OLD CENTRAL PARK RESERVOIR, 1931

When the old reservoir was drained, squatters established a colony on the site. Eventually this wasteland was turned into the pristine grassy oval of the Great Lawn, where ball games were played and picnickers could recline in the sunshine. Landscape designer Olmsted claimed Central Park "is of great importance as the first real park made in this country—a democratic development of the highest significance and on the success of which in my opinion, much of the progress of art and aesthetic culture in this country is dependent." (EVERETT COLLECTION)

SKATING IN FRONT OF THE DAKOTA, 1898

Ice-skating has always been a favorite leisure-time activity for New Yorkers, with one annual park report estimating that approximately 40,000 people visited the ice-covered lakes and ponds in one day. This rented skate chair is being pushed on the lake in front of one of New York's most famous apartment buildings, the Dakota. (THE BYRON COLLECTION/MUSEUM OF THE CITY OF NEW YORK)

CENTRAL PARK RESERVOIR, CA. 1900

The Central Park Reservoir was the main receiving location for the Croton Aqueduct, with the water then piped down to the Croton Reservoir on Fifth Avenue and 42nd Street. A bridle path and a walking path surrounded the vast lake that spread almost the width of the park. North of the reservoir, Central Park was landscaped to conform to its rugged, natural state. (ROBERT L. BRACKLOW/COLLECTION OF THE NEW-YORK HISTORICAL SOCIETY)

COLUMBUS CIRCLE ON THE CORNER OF CENTRAL PARK, CA. 1900

Columbus Circle, at the southwest corner of Central Park, was originally planned as a public speaking space, but the volume of traffic prevented it. The trolley tracks ran down Central Park West and curved around the circle's 80-foot central column topped by a statue of Christopher Columbus. The two-story building at the junction of Broadway and Central Park West was Durland's Riding Academy, one of the largest equestrian schools in the world. (COLLECTION OF THE NEW-YORK HISTORICAL SOCIETY)

WEST END AVENUE FARMS AT 94TH STREET, CA. 1890 (above)

Prior to the 1880s, the Upper West Side consisted of farms and country estates, with sections of the Hudson shore north of 42nd Street lined with the shanties of squatters driven from Central Park. But the arrival of the elevated railroad changed everything. By 1895, there were nearly 80 excavations for buildings under way in the area. The NEW YORK DAILY TRIBUNE reported that "the unequaled views, pure air, solid foundations and proximity to the city's pleasure grounds offer substantial inducements for residential settlement." (ROBERT L. BRACKLOW/COLLECTION OF THE NEW-YORK HISTORICAL SOCIETY)

SOUTH FROM THE DAKOTA, 1890 (facing, above)

This photograph was taken from the Dakota Apartments, completed in 1884 at West 72nd Street and Central Park West. The surrounding area was home to pig farms and shanties. The Dakota was so far from the city, New Yorkers claimed they might as well be in the Dakota territory. But the luxury apartments were a success, ensuring that Central Park West was developed with a series of lavish apartment buildings rather than single-family mansions like those on Fifth Avenue. (MUSEUM OF THE CITY OF NEW YORK)

BLOOMINGDALE ROAD, 1862 (facing, below)

The Upper West Side from 59th to 135th Street was originally known as Bloemendael, the name of a town in the Netherlands. Beginning in 1703, Bloomingdale Road was one of the main routes leaving Manhattan, and by 1795 it ran from Union Square to link up with the old Kingsbridge Road in Westchester County. In 1899 the name of the road was changed to Broadway. (MUSEUM OF THE CITY OF NEW YORK)

THE AMERICAN MUSEUM OF NATURAL HISTORY (above)

The American Museum of Natural History is one of the world's largest institutions devoted to natural science exhibits. The museum is also a research laboratory, a publishing house for scientific manuscripts, and the sponsor of field exploration. It opened in 1869 in the New York Arsenal, and the first grand exhibit hall was completed in 1877 in a wild, rocky area of the West Side, off Central Park West at 77th Street. Additional halls and annexes were added, eventually expanding the complex to include the Hayden Planetarium at 81st Street in 1935. (MUSEUM OF THE CITY OF NEW YORK)

BROADWAY AND AMSTERDAM AVENUE (facing, above)

This photograph of 72nd Street shows Sherman Square, where Broadway crosses Amsterdam Avenue in the foreground; the Ansonia Hotel is at the top-left of the picture. "From Columbus Circle to 181st Street," reported THE WPA GUIDE TO NYC, "Broadway is simply the main street of a large and prosperous residential district. Hundreds of thousands of shoppers, movie-goers, diners, and strollers, whose homes are in the phalanxed apartment buildings and hotels nearby, crowd this wide thoroughfare." (ARCHIVE PHOTOS)

FISH FLOAT IN MACY'S THANKSGIVING DAY PARADE, 1941 (facing, below)

Macy's annual Thanksgiving Day Parade has been a New York City tradition for several generations. The parade features fantastic balloon creatures filled with helium that sail high above the street. The final float always carries Santa Claus, who.waves to the watching children, signaling the beginning of the Christmas shopping season. In this photograph, a flying fish swings from Central Park West onto Broadway to continue the parade downtown. (EVERETT COLLECTION)

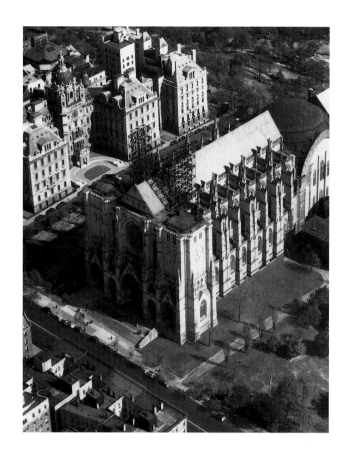

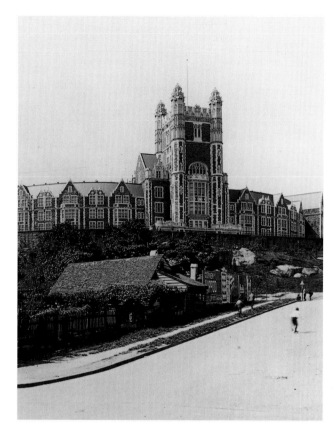

CATHEDRAL OF ST. JOHN THE DIVINE, 1941 (above, left)

This photograph was taken from an airplane, showing the temporary dome that covers the crossing of St. John the Divine. In the Middle Ages it commonly took generations of artisans and workmen to build the local cathedral. Similarly, St. John the Divine is now more than a century old and is still under construction. The cornerstone of the Mother Church of the Episcopal diocese of New York was laid in 1892 on the ridge of Morningside Heights, at Amsterdam Avenue and West 112th Street. The nave is more than 600 feet long and is uniquely designed with the buttresses on the inside of the granite walls. Even unfinished, St. John's is the largest cathedral in the world, since technically St. Peter's in Rome is a church. (EVERETT COLLECTION)

CITY COLLEGE AT 140TH STREET, 1909 (above, right)

Below the City College building, the old house on Convent Avenue was torn down a few months after this photograph was taken. City College was established in 1849 as a "Free Academy" for pupils who had attended the common schools and could pass the entrance examinations. New York City was committed to the liberal ideal of a free college education for all citizens. The main center of City College was established shortly after the turn of the century on a ridge of land stretching from 136th to 140th Street. (ROBERT L. BRACKLOW/COLLECTION OF THE NEW-YORK HISTORICAL SOCIETY)

SOLDIERS AND SAILORS MONUMENT ON RIVERSIDE DRIVE, 1938 (facing)

Riverside Park was established along the Hudson River from West 72nd Street to the northern tip of Manhattan (with a break between 125th and 135th Streets). The park was built in English pastoral style, with a rustic retaining wall, meandering paths, and informally arranged landscaping. This photograph of the Memorial Day Parade shows the Seventh Regiment passing a reviewing stand at the Soldiers and Sailors Monument on 89th Street and Riverside Drive. The monument was completed in 1902 to honor the Union fighters in the Civil War. Thirty-three blocks further north in Riverside Park is the beautiful domed tomb of Ulysses S. Grant. Grant asked to be buried in New York "because the people of that city befriended me in my need." (EVERETT COLLECTION)

HOUSES ON WEST 133RD STREET, CA. 1880
Harlem was a remote village for two centuries, but after the extension of the elevated railroads in the 1880s, the area was actively developed. Tenements and apartment houses were built along the streets. Ten years after this photograph was taken, the vacant lots were almost completely filled in with similar brick buildings. The nearby Polo Grounds and the 1889 opening of Oscar Hammerstein's Harlem Opera House on 125th Street helped spur the development of respectable housing on the northern half of Manhattan island. (COLLECTION OF THE NEW-YORK HISTORICAL SOCIETY)

125TH STREET IN HARLEM
This photograph is looking west toward Eighth Avenue down 125th Street, the main business thoroughfare in Harlem. The Apollo Theater on the right was famous as Harlem's musical showcase. The boundary of Harlem was roughly from 110th to 155th Street, stretching from the East River to Morningside Avenue. (ARCHIVE PHOTOS)

CHILDREN RIDING STREETCAR, CA. 1930S

The first electric streetcars appeared at the turn of the century. In 1919, streetcars carried more passengers than the elevated lines and the subways. Streetcars were eventually replaced with buses and the Third Avenue line was closed in the late 1930s. (COLLECTION OF THE NATIONAL ARHIVES)

MARCUS GARVEY

Marcus Garvey founded the Universal Negro Improvement Association in Jamaica in 1914, and brought it to Harlem several years later. He published a weekly called the NEGRO WORLD in which he urged Negro unity, nationalism, and the resettlement of blacks in Africa. A skilled orator, Garvey sparked the first mass civil movement among African-Americans. In 1923, thousands of people were loyal to Garvey when he was convicted by a politically motivated federal court of using the mails to defraud. He was deported in 1927 to Jamaica. (ARCHIVE PHOTOS)

HARLEM STREET SCENE, 1939

By 1930, the black population in Manhattan was 300,000, with over 200,000 living in Harlem. Each part of Harlem was self-contained, in distinct neighborhoods such as Sugar Hill, the Valley, Manhattanville, Strivers' Row, Bradhurst, and Hamilton Heights. Sharp divisions separated the middle class from the affluent and the destitute. (SID GROSSMAN/MUSEUM OF THE CITY OF NEW YORK)

LIONEL HAMPTON PLAYING THE VIBRAPHONE, 1937 (above, left)
Lionel Hampton was an orchestra leader and a brilliant improviser on the vibraphone. Hampton first experimented with the electrically amplified instrument in October 1930 in jam sessions with Louis Armstrong. From 1936 to 1940 he became famous as a member of Benny Goodman's jazz quartet. (FRANK DRIGGS COLLECTION/ARCHIVE PHOTOS)

BILLIE HOLIDAY, CA. 1935 (above, right)
Billie Holiday wrote in her 1956 autobiography, "I opened Café Society as an unknown; I left two years later as a star." Her beautiful tone and expressive delivery made her one of the most important jazz singers in America. Despite her stardom, Holiday still had to use the service elevator when she stayed at the Waldorf-Astoria Hotel. (FRANK DRIGGS COLLECTION/ARCHIVE PHOTOS)

THE COTTON CLUB, CA. 1928 (facing)
After World War I, downtown folk were drawn to Harlem by the lure of nightclubs like the Cotton Club on 133rd Street, Small's at 135th Street, and the Big Apple on Seventh Avenue. Harlem nightlife had a reputation for being cosmopolitan because it was popular among artists, writers, and foreign visitors. Patrons packed the clubs to drink illegal whiskey during Prohibition and to hear swing and jazz music by artists such as Lionel Hampton, Cab Calloway, Duke Ellington, Louis Armstrong, Jimmie Lunceford, and Ella Fitzgerald. In 1936 the Cotton Club moved to Times Square to capitalize on its success. (FRANK DRIGGS COLLECTION/ARCHIVE PHOTOS)

AUTO-GYROS OVER THE GEORGE WASHINGTON BRIDGE, 1930
Two auto-gyros fly over the span of the George Washington Bridge shortly before the roadway was attached, joining Manhattan with New Jersey. The auto-gyros were traveling from Pitcairn Airfield in Willow Grove, Pennsylvania, to New York City to map the wind currents among the tall buildings. They also scouted possible landing sites on and among the structures. (NATIONAL ARCHIVES)

GEORGE WASHINGTON BRIDGE UNDER CONSTRUCTION, 1930
The building project to complete the magnificent George Washington Bridge over the Hudson River lasted from 1926 to 1931. The bridge was 3,500 feet long, more than twice the length of the Brooklyn Bridge. The arched towers were originally intended to be faced in granite, but the steel construction was considered graceful and pleasing enough to be left bare. It was also more cost-effective to forgo the stone facing. The bridge was built and operated by the Port of New York Authority as part of the system of bridges and tunnels attempting to solve the transportation problems of Manhattan and its neighbors. (ARCHIVE PHOTOS)

OPENING-DAY TRAFFIC ACROSS GEORGE WASHINGTON BRIDGE, OCTOBER 25, 1931
This photograph captures the first traffic jam at the George Washington Bridge, taken on opening day, looking toward New Jersey. During 1937, approximately eight million vehicles paid tolls to cross the bridge. (ARCHIVE PHOTOS)

BALLOONING DURING THE HARLEM RIVER BOAT RACES

The Harlem River was beautiful at the turn of the century, with pretty inlets where small craft could anchor. The grassy vistas and points were used as pleasure grounds, with country clubs and old mansions gracing the shoreline. (ROBERT L. BRACKLOW/MUSEUM OF THE CITY OF NEW YORK)

OPENING OF THE HARLEM RIVER SHIP CANAL, JUNE 17, 1895

Before the ship canal was built, the Harlem River could be forded by jumping from rock to rock at the Spuyten Duyvil Creek. City engineers dredged the Harlem 15 feet deep and up to 400 feet wide, creating a continuous waterway between the Hudson and East Rivers. Crowds gathered near 155th Street to watch the first steamship chug down the channel. (THE BYRON COLLECTION/MUSEUM OF THE CITY OF NEW YORK)

INWOOD HEIGHTS, MAGDALEN HOUSE, SOUTH FROM DYCKMAN STREET, 1933

At the northern tip of Manhattan, Inwood Heights offered spectacular views of the Hudson River and the New Jersey Palisades. In 1938 the Cloisters opened in Fort Tyron Park, which covered nearly half of Inwood Heights. (ROBERT L. BRACKLOW/MUSEUM OF THE CITY OF NEW YORK)

B O

WASHINGTON BRIDGE UNDER CONSTRUCTION, 1888
(NORMAN WURTS/MUSEUM OF THE CITY OF NEW YORK)

OUTER

ROUGHS

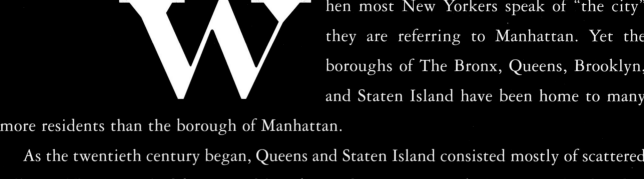

W hen most New Yorkers speak of "the city" they are referring to Manhattan. Yet the boroughs of The Bronx, Queens, Brooklyn, and Staten Island have been home to many more residents than the borough of Manhattan.

As the twentieth century began, Queens and Staten Island consisted mostly of scattered villages. The Bronx had been steadily subsumed into New York City over the decades; several Bronx townships were added in 1874, and in 1895 three more were taken in. Brooklyn was in its own right the third largest city in the United States.

Greater New York was born in 1898. The new city charter made each borough a political subdivision of the city that would elect its own president. New York City was now 320 square miles in area, easily the biggest and most populous city in America.

The Bronx lies north of Manhattan and is the city's only mainland borough. It was named for the first Danish immigrant who settled there, Jonas Bronck. The Bronx was basically 42 square miles of residential neighborhoods that featured a public park even larger than Central Park.

Queens was physically the largest borough and consisted of more than a third of the city's total area, covering about 120 square miles. The land on the northern half of Long Island was first settled in 1635 by the Dutch, who established themselves on Flushing Bay, a shallow inlet of the East River.

Brooklyn was the most populated borough. It consisted of 81 square miles, containing the remnants of 25 villages that eventually merged into one continuous metropolis. As a maritime and industrial center, Brooklyn was fifth in the nation in manufacturing.

Staten Island is an island covering 60 square miles, south of Manhattan, closer to New Jersey than to the rest of the city. Staten Island has always been the least developed and least densely populated borough of New York City, and retained its rural character well into the mid-twentieth century.

BRONX

HIGH BRIDGE AND WATER TOWER
Connecting Manhattan island with the mainland of The Bronx, High Bridge is the oldest of New York's bridges over the Harlem River,
constructed from 1837 to 1848. When the bridge was new, Edgar Allan Poe frequently strolled along the pedestrian walkway for the view
114 feet above the tidewater. The Roman-style bridge was built as part of the Croton Aqueduct system, which brought water into
Manhattan, with the High Bridge Tower on the right used to equalize the water pressure in the reservoir. (THE J. CLARENCE DAVIES
COLLECTION/MUSEUM OF THE CITY OF NEW YORK)

LEXINGTON AVENUE ELEVATED SUBWAY LINE, THE BRONX, 1909
This street had been recently paved as part of the expanding services for New York City's outer boroughs after the incorporation of New York City in 1898. The elevated subway line rises above Westchester Avenue as it crosses Rogers Place. Across the foreground runs Dongan Street, later designated as 163rd Street. The connection of the subway and the Third Avenue El encouraged hundreds of thousands of people to leave tenements in Manhattan and move to The Bronx. (THE BRONX COUNTY HISTORICAL SOCIETY)

PERRY AVENUE NEAR 205TH STREET, 1913
Perry Avenue was paved in 1911 when substantial frame houses flanked the quiet street. It was favorably situated between Van Cortlandt Park and the New York Botanical Gardens. One of the first motor cars in The Bronx is parked beside the curb. (THE BRONX COUNTY HISTORICAL SOCIETY)

FORDHAM UNIVERSITY PARADE GROUND, 1910 (above)

Fordham University was founded as St. John's College in 1841, and five years later became a Jesuit-run college. The stone buildings are scattered over a large campus: On the right is Hughes Hall, the Fordham Prep school; Dealy Hall is on the left, a residence and classroom building for Fordham; and in the center is the Administration Building. Fordham University's parade ground was one of the centers of college activities, used for sports and parades of the corps of cadets. (THE BRONX COUNTY HISTORICAL SOCIETY)

GRAND CONCOURSE LOOKING NORTHEAST FROM 192ND STREET, CA. 1925 (facing, above)

The Grand Concourse runs nearly five miles through the center of The Bronx. It was originally conceived of for upwardly mobile residents, and was considered to be the Park Avenue of The Bronx. It was lined with elegant apartment buildings. The thoroughfare is 180 feet wide and also served as the parade route for the borough. The trees to the right are Edgar Allan Poe Park, with the cottage in which the poet lived from 1846 to 1849 set back from the boulevard. (THE BRONX COUNTY HISTORICAL SOCIETY)

THE BRONX ZOO, 1904 (facing, below)

The Bronx Park rivaled Central Park with its 662 acres of forest, meadows, hills, and vista points. Along with the Botanical Gardens, the park featured the largest zoo in America, the New York Zoological Society, more commonly known as the Bronx Zoo. When they established the zoo in 1899, the founders stated they wanted to make "captive animals not only comfortable but really happy." In this photograph, the sea lions lounge on warm rocks in a fenced-in pen. Behind the pen is the famous Reptile House. (MUSEUM OF THE CITY OF NEW YORK)

BABE RUTH AT YANKEE STADIUM, 1934
The home of the "winningest team" in baseball history was
Yankee Stadium, opened at 161st Street in 1923. The
75,000-seat stadium was the largest baseball park in the
United States before World War II. The Yankees became
known as the "Bronx Bombers" because of the legendary
home runs hit by such players as Babe Ruth, Lou Gehrig,
and Joe DiMaggio. In this photograph, Babe Ruth bids
farewell to his teammates and his fans as he leaves the
Yankees. He finished his career with the Boston Braves
in 1935. (HOWARD H. MULLER COLLECTION/ARCHIVE PHOTOS)

QUEENS

TRIBOROUGH BRIDGE, 1937
The Triborough Bridge links together the boroughs of Manhattan, Queens, and The Bronx. Construction began on October 25, 1929. Work on the bridge was stopped due to a lack of funds until the Public Works Administration granted the city $9 million and bought $35 million in bridge bonds. Finally completed in July 1936, the bridge is a vertical lift structure that is tall enough to allow sailing ships to pass underneath.
(BERENICE ABBOTT/MUSEUM OF THE CITY OF NEW YORK)

LONG ISLAND CITY

Long Island City lay directly across the East River from Midtown Manhattan, and was second only to Jamaica as a business center in Queens. After the Queensboro Bridge was opened in 1909, new streets were established and a large number of houses were built to accommodate new residents. According to THE WPA GUIDE TO NYC, "In 1938 Queens had 1,700 industrial establishments, 5 percent of the city's total. More than 1,400 are crowded into a 2.8-square-mile area of Long Island City. It is said that drab and oily Newtown Creek carries more freight annually than the Mississippi River." (ARCHIVE PHOTOS)

JAMAICA AT 160TH STREET, CA. 1900

Jamaica dates back to 1656, when it was settled by English colonists. Because of its proximity to Manhattan and Brooklyn, Jamaica became a trading center for the farmers of Long Island. It continued to grow rapidly with the arrival of the Long Island Railroad in 1836, a line for the electric trolley in 1888, and the extension of the subways in 1920. Jamaica became known as a significant shopping district. Parceled between 160th and 168th streets, the avenue had the highest relative assessed valuation in Queens between 1920 and 1940. (QUEENS HISTORICAL SOCIETY)

ROOSEVELT AVENUE EAST AT MAIN STREET IN FLUSHING, QUEENS, 1944 (above)

Flushing developed as a residential community after trolley lines were extended during the 1890s and the subway lines appeared in 1928. Main Street was the prime business, shopping, and public service center. As in the rest of Queens, most of the homes in Flushing were one- or two-family dwellings well into the twentieth century. (QUEENS HISTORICAL SOCIETY)

BOWNE AVENUE AND AMITY STREET IN FLUSHING, QUEENS, CA. 1880 (facing)

Flushing, east of the Flushing River, was one of New York's wealthiest summer colonies by the mid-nineteenth century, with wide tree-lined streets and rows of wooden houses. Flushing was founded in 1654 by Dutch colonists who called it Vlissingen. In 1657, English Quakers arrived under promise of religious tolerance by Governor Peter Stuyvesant. John Bowne wrote the Flushing Remonstrance, which was approved at a town meeting; it is considered one of the earliest documents proclaiming religious freedom in America. (QUEENS HISTORICAL SOCIETY)

NIGHT DIVER AT THE WORLD'S FAIR, 1939

The modern design of the 1939 World's Fair reflected its theme—the World of Tomorrow. With tensions high in Europe and refugees pouring into New York City, the theme was a plea of hope on the eve of World War II. Exhibitors included about 60 countries and 33 states and territories. Among the products introduced to the public at this World's Fair were television, air-conditioning, color film, nylon stockings, and diesel engines. When war broke out, the theme was changed to "For Peace and Freedom." (HOWARD W. FRANK COLLECTION)

WORLD'S FAIR IN FLUSHING, 1939

Flushing Meadow was a city dump on the edge of Corona when Robert Moses chose it as the site of the 1939 World's Fair. The extensive network of buildings and parkways rested on landfill. Dominating the World's Fair was the 700-foot-high Trylon and the 200-foot-wide Perisphere placed at the heart of the Theme Center, seen here at the top of the photo. (EVERETT COLLECTION)

LA GUARDIA AIRPORT

New York City stood at the dawn of the air age when its second municipal airport opened in 1939, just in time to serve visitors to the World's Fair. Originally called North Beach Airport, it was renamed La Guardia after New York City's favorite mayor, who was an enthusiastic advocate of aviation. The land and seaplane terminal was built on landfill extending into Flushing Bay. The cost of construction, nearly $45 million, was paid by the WPA. La Guardia became the city's major cargo and passenger airport due to its close proximity to Manhattan. (MUSEUM OF THE CITY OF NEW YORK)

AT THE RACES IN BELMONT PARK, ELMONT, L.I., 1939

Racing fans crowded the rails at Belmont track even during the middle of the workday. According to THE WPA GUIDE TO NYC: "The smooth terrain of this part of Long Island, first known as the 'Plains,' has attracted race courses ever since horse racing was introduced into the colonies in 1665. The Belmont Park track, whose western gates are just within the Queens boundary, serves to keep alive this tradition in the neighborhood." (HOWARD W. FRANK COLLECTION)

BROOKLYN

PEDESTRIANS ON THE PROMENADE OF THE BROOKLYN BRIDGE, CA. 1910

The Brooklyn Bridge was completed in 1883, and a decade later HARPER'S described the 12-foot-wide promenade at 5 P.M.: "Thirty thousand men, women, and children are in the torrent, 30,000 pedestrians in a 90-minute downpour." In the late evening, it was a favorite place for couples to go for a romantic stroll, looking at the lights of Manhattan and Brooklyn. The Brooklyn Bridge became a cultural icon and a symbol of American industrial power, inspiring many writers and artists. (NATIONAL ARCHIVES, PICTURES OF THE AMERICAN CITY)

PANORAMA OF THE BROOKLYN BRIDGE, CA. 1905

The design and construction of the Brooklyn Bridge was one of the greatest engineering feats in the world. Opened in 1883, the bridge was the lifework of two generations of the Roebling family. Engineer John A. Roebling was a German immigrant who designed the bridge to be twice as long as any other in existence. In 1869, while Roebling was surveying the location for the main towers, his foot was crushed by a docking ferry and he subsequently died of lockjaw. His son, Washington A. Roebling, then became chief engineer of the project. In December 1871, the younger Roebling contracted the bends while helping to fight a fire that had started in the underwater caisson of the Brooklyn tower. After he suffered a second attack in the New York caisson, Roebling was an invalid for the rest of his life. With the help of his wife Emily Warren Roebling, who was also trained in engineering, they were able to complete the Brooklyn Bridge. Emily became the field marshal at the site while her husband sat in a wheelchair in their Brooklyn Heights home, overseeing and observing the construction through a telescope. (GEORGE P. HALL & SON/COLLECTION OF THE NEW-YORK HISTORICAL SOCIETY)

CONSTRUCTION OF THE BROOKLYN BRIDGE, CA. 1877

During the construction of the Brooklyn Bridge, the footpath slung from the main cables was open for a small fee, but the number of tourists soon became too great, and the practice had to be stopped. Workmen grumbled at being called from their duties to assist terrified people, immobilized with fear from the swinging of the footbridge and the dizzying height. (ARCHIVE PHOTOS)

FULTON FERRY HOUSE (above)
The first ferry from Brooklyn to Manhattan was established in 1642. Ferries were usually rowboats or sailing scows, and it was not unusual for boats to capsize in the strong winds. Robert Fulton introduced steam-powered ferryboats in 1814, traveling between Fulton Street in Brooklyn and Fulton Street in Manhattan. The Fulton Ferry carried more than 100,000 passengers a day by the mid-nineteenth century. It went into a decline after 1883 when the Brooklyn Bridge was built. The last ferry crossed the river in 1924. (ARCHIVE PHOTOS)

FIRE AT THE BROOKLYN DOCKS, 1941 (facing, above)
In this photograph, fireboats fight a fire following a series of explosions on the Cuba Mail Line pier. The fire swept out of control through the Brooklyn waterfront. Two men were killed and considerable property damage occurred. (MUSEUM OF THE CITY OF NEW YORK)

BROOKLYN NAVY YARDS (facing, below)
In 1800, the U.S. government began to build Navy yards on 200 acres of Wallabout Bay, a semicircular bay in the East River between the Williamsburg and Manhattan Bridges. The world-famous Navy Yards included shipyards, cranes, foundries, machine shops, warehouses, barracks, a power plant, and a railroad spur. Factories and housing for the workers sprang up around the busy yard. (MUSEUM OF THE CITY OF NEW YORK)

PROSPECT LAKE IN PROSPECT PARK

Prospect Park was designed and built right after the Civil War by Central Park architects Frederick Law Olmsted and Calvert Vaux. The park was part of the general expansion of Brooklyn's municipal features during the post–Civil War economic boom. Prospect Park was 526 acres of scenic bluffs and wooded meadows, with Prospect Lake winding picturesquely into the middle of the park. By the turn of the century, there were as many as 15 million visitors a year. (ARCHIVE PHOTOS)

BROOKLYN HEIGHTS, 1877

Many prominent merchant families built their homes on Brooklyn Heights, a bluff facing the East River. Brooklyn Heights has always been a distinctive residential area because of the dramatic views it offers of New York Harbor. This photograph shows two famous mansions on Pierrepont Place, so named because the first house was owned by Henry Pierrepont. The double brownstone to the right was designed by Richard Upjohn in 1856 for the merchants A. A. Low and A. M. White. (MUSEUM OF THE CITY OF NEW YORK)

FROM BOROUGH HALL, LOOKING UP FULTON STREET, 1892 (above)

Fulton Street is Brooklyn's oldest thoroughfare and was first known as the Old Ferry Road. In the colonial days it was called the King's Highway, and was renamed in the nineteenth century in honor of Robert Fulton. Fulton Street downtown was the main street of Brooklyn: a nexus of subways, streetcars, and elevated lines providing access to county and borough government buildings, and to business, shopping, and theater establishments. (MUSEUM OF THE CITY OF NEW YORK)

BOROUGH HALL PLAZA, 1927 (facing)

The Borough Hall Plaza is at the convergence of Court, Fulton, and Joralemon Streets. Public buildings were on Joralemon Street, while Court Street was the home of banks and real estate firms. Many of Brooklyn's institutions of higher learning were in the area: Long Island University, Brooklyn Law School, and St. John's University. This photograph was taken at a slow shutter speed, which resulted in blurs from anyone or anything that moved. (THE BROOKLYN PUBLIC LIBRARY)

FLOYD BENNETT FIELD, 1933

Floyd Bennett Field was finished in 1930 and was the city's first municipal airport. In this photograph, a crowd waits for the arrival of James Mollison and his wife Amy Johnson on their transatlantic flight from Wales. (EVERETT COLLECTION)

EBBETS FIELD, 1942

In this photograph, the Brooklyn Dodgers play the Chicago Cubs in a twilight game in Ebbets Field in Flatbush. The Brooklyn baseball team got their name from "trolley dodgers," the term used for Brooklynites who dodged the fast electric streetcars. (ARCHIVE PHOTOS)

LOOKING NORTHWARD ALONG FLATBUSH AVENUE, CA. 1880

On the left is a colonial house built by Jeremiah Lott. Flatbush was still rural in 1880. (THE BROOKLYN PUBLIC LIBRARY)

GREEN-WOOD CEMETERY, CA. 1880 (above)

"I must now give a brief account of Green-Wood Cemetery, which we visited the other day," wrote Lady Emmeline Stuart Wortley in TRAVELS IN THE UNITED STATES (1851). "The views from the heights of the cemetery were sublime. I admired the one from Ocean Hill the most. There is a lovely variety of valleys, elevations, plains, groves, glades, and paths. When will London have anything even approaching this magnificent cemetery? The ocean rolling and moaning, with its fine melancholy, organ-like sounds, so near, like a mighty mourner." (COLLECTION OF THE NEW-YORK HISTORICAL SOCIETY)

GERRITTSEN BEACH, BROOKLYN (facing, above)

On the Rockaway Inlet, Gerrittsen Beach remained unchanged for centuries. The area was named for Wolfert Gerrittsen, who built a house and mill there in the seventeenth century. A summer resort was built in 1920 consisting of rows of bungalows with peaked roofs. (ARCHIVE PHOTOS)

GOWANUS CANAL (facing, below)

Located on the Brooklyn coast behind Governors Island, Gowanus Bay was among the first land acquisitions the Dutch made from Native Americans. With the construction of the Gowanus Canal in the 1840s, the bay became one of the most intensively developed areas of the waterfront, with shipyards and warehouses connected by extensive railway tracks. Sailors from around the world filled the bars and rooming houses of Red Hook and Gowanus. (ARCHIVE PHOTOS)

BRIGHTON BEACH HOTEL BEING PULLED AWAY FROM THE OCEAN, 1890

Brighton Beach is on the east side of Coney Island, and was named in 1878 after the famous sea resort in England. By 1888, the Hotel Brighton was threatened with the encroaching waves of the Atlantic. The 500-foot-wide hotel was jacked up and placed on 120 flatcars running on railroad tracks, and six steam engines moved it inland. (COLLECTION OF THE NEW-YORK HISTORICAL SOCIETY)

SURF AVENUE ON CONEY ISLAND, 1895

Surf Avenue was the main thoroughfare of Coney Island. In this photograph, most of the small buildings across the street are bathing pavilions, food stands, penny arcades, or game booths. Coney Island had a plethora of freak shows, fun houses, carousels, dance halls, penny arcades, waxworks, shooting galleries, souvenir shops, and horse-racing, boxing, and food establishments. Some popular innovations included frankfurters, roller coasters, and mixed public bathing. "A ride on the camel . . . is another 'superb sensation' not to be despised," reported the METROPOLITAN MAGAZINE in 1897, adding that "for the munificent sum of two dollars one can taste to the utmost limits the dissipations of Coney Island." (THE BYRON COLLECTION/MUSEUM OF THE CITY OF NEW YORK)

CONEY ISLAND BEACH, 1936

With the extension of the subway lines in the 1920s, Coney Island became accessible to millions of lower-income New Yorkers. Summer crowds filled Coney Island, drawn to the fun of the amusement parks and the nearby racetracks. Immigrants on ships inbound from Europe reported they could see the giant illuminated Ferris wheel at Coney Island long before they caught sight of the Statue of Liberty. (ARCHIVE PHOTOS)

PICNICKING ON CONEY ISLAND BEACH, 1896

Before the turn of the century, people remained in their street clothes when they were on the beach. THE ILLUSTRATED AMERICAN of 1892 bemoaned the advent of the bathing suit: "Students of human nature have sought in vain for an explanation of the utter rout of supposedly ingrained sentiments and conventionalities that attends the donning of a bathing suit." (THE BYRON COLLECTION/MUSEUM OF THE CITY OF NEW YORK)

LUNA PARK AT NIGHT, CONEY ISLAND, CA. 1910

Luna Park was an amusement park created by Frederick Thompson and Elmer Dundy in 1903. The park drew more than 90,000 people a day to its rides, theatrical shows, huge saltwater swimming pool, and spacious ballroom. At night, the park was lit with more than a million incandescent bulbs. It was destroyed by fire in 1911. (ARCHIVE PHOTOS)

STATEN ISLAND

STATEN ISLAND FERRY IN THE MIST, 1934

White clouds of mist rise from the waters of the bay on February 9, 1934, the coldest day in over a century. The Staten Island Ferry was known for its picturesque journey between the smaller islands of Upper New York Bay. The five miles between Manhattan and Staten Island offer a panoramic view of Lower Manhattan, Brooklyn, and New Jersey during the half-hour trip. It was a sightseeing bargain for tourists visiting the city. (EVERETT COLLECTION)

STATEN ISLAND LOOKING OVER NEW YORK BAY TO MANHATTAN, 1897

Todt Hill is more than 400 feet tall, the highest elevation found along the New York Bay coastline. This photograph looks across the neighborhoods of Staten Island and over Upper New York Bay, with Manhattan in the distance. Staten Island could only be reached by ferry from Manhattan and Brooklyn; thus it remained comparatively rural, though it was part of the largest city in America. (AUGUST LOEFFLER/COLLECTION OF THE NEW-YORK HISTORICAL SOCIETY)

FROM THE STATEN ISLAND FERRY AS IT PULLS AWAY FROM THE SLIPS

The first municipal ferry service was established in 1905, with the St. George Ferry carrying most of the island's working population back and forth to Manhattan. The earliest ferry service was a sailboat operated by Cornelius "Commodore" Vanderbilt in 1810, when he was only 16 years old, for transporting farm produce and passengers. St. George was still rural in the 1830s, but by the turn of the century, it was the civic, business, cultural, and transit center of Staten Island. (ARCHIVE PHOTOS)

STATEN ISLAND, INTERSECTION OF CENTRAL AVENUE AND BAY STREET
On Staten Island, the hilly inland region abuts the flat plain of the eastern shoreline, where some of the island's oldest communities are located.
On the left are several nineteenth-century gabled mansions typical of those built on Staten Island in an era when wood and labor were cheap.
(P. L. SPERR/ARCHIVE PHOTOS)

SAILOR'S SNUG HARBOR, CA. 1900
Sailor's Snug Harbor was an organization to aid indigent seamen, founded in 1801 when the son of a privateer bequeathed most of his fortune
to the establishment of a retirement home. The home for "aged, decrepit, and worn-out sailors" was established in 1831 on an estate overlook-
ing the Kill van Kull (running between New Jersey and Staten Island). Mariners who could prove they had spent at least five years at sea were
provided with food, shelter, tobacco, and entertainment. By 1900, 1,000 seamen lived in the vast complex. (THE BYRON COLLECTION/MUSEUM OF
THE CITY OF NEW YORK)

EPILOGUE

KISS IN TIMES SQUARE, 1945

Nearly 500,000 people filled Times Square on August 14, 1945, when the New York Times Building flashed the official word from President Truman that the Japanese had surrendered. The following month, LIFE magazine published this photograph of a sailor giving a nurse a heartfelt kiss in Times Square on V-J Day. The image became famous across America, capturing the exuberance at the end of the war and heralding the beginning of the peacetime era. With the end of the war, America became a world superpower, and New York City took its place as the center of development for postwar prosperity. (ALFRED EISENSTAEDT/LIFE MAGAZINE, TIME INC.)

Selected Bibliography

Andrews, Wayne. *Architecture in New York.* New York: Harper & Row, 1969.

Barlow, Elizabeth, and Alex, William. *Frederick Law Olmsted's New York.* New York: Praeger, in association with the Whitney Museum of American Art, 1972.

Burnham, Alan, ed. *New York Landmarks.* Middletown, Connecticut: Wesleyan University Press, 1963.

Churchill, Allen. *The Improper Bohemians: Greenwich Village in Its Heyday.* New York: Dutton, 1959.

Churchill, Allen. *The Upper Crust.* Englewood Cliffs, New Jersey: Prentice-Hall, 1970.

Davis, Elmer. *History of the New York Times, 1851–1921.* New York: The New York Times, 1921.

Delaney, Edmund T., and Charles Lockwood. *Greenwich Village: A Photographic Guide.* New York: Dover, 1976.

Dickens, Charles. *American Notes for General Circulation.* New York: Longmans Green, 1957.

Ellis, Edward Robb. *The Epic of New York City.* New York: Kodansha America Inc., 1997.

Federal Writers' Project of the Works Progress Administration for the City of New York. *The WPA Guide to New York City.* New York: Random House, 1939.

Feininger, Andreas; text by John von Hartz. *New York in the Forties.* New York: Dover, 1978.

The Fifth Avenue Association. *Fifty Years on Fifth.* New York: International Press, 1957.

Five Borough Street Guide to New York City. New York: Geographia Map Co., 1962.

Glazer, Nathan, and Moynihan, Daniel Patrick. *Beyond the Melting Pot.* Cambridge: M.I.T. Press and Harvard University Press, 1963.

Goldstone, Harmon H., and Dalrymple, Martha. *History Preserved: A Guide to New York City Landmarks and Historic Districts.* New York: Simon & Schuster, 1974.

Harper's Magazine. *New York: A Collection from Harper's Magazine.* New York: Gallery Books, 1991.

Hawkins, Stuart. *New York, New York.* New York: Wilfred Funk, 1957.

Jackson, Kenneth T. *The Encyclopedia of New York City.* New Haven: Yale University Press, 1995.

James, Rian. *All About New York.* New York: Day, 1931.

Johnson, James Weldon. *Black Manhattan.* New York: Arno Press, 1968, or Knopf, 1930.

Kouwenhoven, John A. *The Columbia Historical Portrait of New York.* New York: Doubleday, 1953.

Lightfoot, Frederick S. *Nineteenth-Century New York in Rare Photographic Views.* New York: Dover, 1981.

Lockwood, Charles. *Manhattan Moves Uptown: An Illustrated History.* New York: Barnes & Noble, 1995.

Longstreet, Stephen. *City on Two Rivers: Profiles of New York—Yesterday and Today.* New York: Hawthorn, 1975.

Mayer, Grace M. *Once Upon a City.* New York: Macmillan, 1958.

Miller, Terry. *Greenwich Village and How it Got that Way.* New York: Crown, 1990.

Morris, Lloyd. *Incredible New York.* New York: Random House, 1951.

Mumford, Lewis. *The Brown Decades.* New York: Dover, 1955.

Nevins, Allan, and Krout, John A., eds. *The Greater City: New York, 1898–1948.* New York: Columbia University Press, 1948.

Riis, Jacob A. *How the Other Half Lives: Studies Among the Tenements of New York.* New York: Sagamore Press, 1957.

Rosen, Laura. *Top of the City: New York's Hidden Rooftop World.* New York: Thames and Hudson, 1982.

Shapiro, Mary J. *A Picture History of the Brooklyn Bridge.* New York: Dover, 1983.

Simon, Kate. *Fifth Avenue: A Very Social History.* New York: Harcourt Brace Jovanovich, 1978.

Thomas, Norman, and Blanshard, Paul. *What's the Matter with New York.* New York: Macmillan, 1932.

Van Dyke, John C. *The New New York.* New York: Macmillan, 1909.

Watson, Edward B. *New York Then and Now.* Photographs by Edmund V. Gillon, Jr. New York: Dover, 1976.

Wharton, Edith. *The Age of Innocence.* New York: Appleton, 1920.

White, E. B. *Here Is New York.* New York: Doubleday Doran, 1939.

Williams, Sherman. *New York's Part in History.* New York: Appleton, 1915.